MW01204301

Lord, he... with the same beauty it had
when it tumbled from your creative hand.
Help me see that
"Nothing here below is profane.
On the contrary, everything is sacred."

— *Pierre Teilhard de Chardin, S.J.*

*Alley of oaks connecting the Academy
of the Sacred Heart with St. Charles
College, planted in 1837*

GRAND COTEAU
The Holy Land of South Louisiana

GRAND COTEAU
The Holy Land of South Louisiana

TRENT ANGERS

Acadian House
PUBLISHING
LAFAYETTE, LOUISIANA

Copyright © 2005 by Trent Angers

All rights reserved, including the right to reproduce this book or portions thereof in any form whatsoever. For information, contact Acadian House Publishing, P.O. Box 52247, Lafayette, Louisiana 70505, or via e-mail: info@acadianhouse.com.

Library of Congress Cataloging-in-Publication Data

Angers, Trent.
Grand Coteau : the Holy Land of South Louisiana / by Trent Angers.— 1st ed.
    p. cm.
Includes bibliographical references and index.
  ISBN 0-925417-47-5
1. Catholic Church—Louisiana—Grand Coteau—History.
2. Sacred space—Louisiana—Grand Coteau—History.
3. Grand Coteau (La.)—Church history. I. Title.
  BX1418.G73A54 2005
  282'.76346—dc22

                          2004023746

♦ Published by Acadian House Publishing, Lafayette, Louisiana
   (Interior graphic design and production by Jon Russo)

♦ Cover design and production by Elizabeth Bell, Lafayette, Louisiana

♦ Printed by Phoenix Color Corp., Rockaway, New Jersey, USA

Preface

Discovering truth and beauty in Grand Coteau

It seems only natural to me that when you love and enjoy a place you want to share it with others. Grand Coteau, Louisiana, is such a place. This book represents an effort to share the beauty and the uniqueness of this holy land in southern Louisiana.

Grand Coteau is a peaceful little town with lots of open space for walking and thinking. It is covered with great oaks and tall pines, and in the spring a profusion of azaleas dresses it in brilliant color. It is free of the noise and busyness of the city, and tranquility is its middle name.

The sunrises here are exceptional, especially in the autumn. They're inspiring and tend to call a person to prayer, particularly while on retreat, away from the hustle and bustle of life. Grand Coteau is a good place to pray what could be called The Prayer of Dawn. The thing about this prayer is that you don't have to say a word, nor make an effort to think, but only be still and watch and know who it is who paints the beautiful colors of dawn.

My involvement with Grand Coteau goes back to the spring of 1976, when I interviewed two elderly religious sisters at the Academy of the Sacred Heart. I was writing an article on the Miracle of Grand Coteau for *Acadiana Profile*, the Lafayette, Louisiana-based magazine of which I was (and am) editor. I was fascinated by the story, enchanted by the wise old sisters, and thoroughly intrigued when they unshelved a stack of documents from the 1860s bearing witness to the miracle that had occurred in the very building in which we were meeting.

I was re-introduced to Grand Coteau in the fall of 1989, when I made my first silent retreat at Our Lady of the Oaks Retreat House. It was, and continues to be, quite an experience: a clean, simple room; lots of wide open space outdoors for meandering about; brief, inspiring talks by the Jesuit retreat director; perfect meals three times a day; a warm sense of camaraderie among the retreatants; and the welcome silence that helps to create an environment in which prayer and reflection easily move beyond the level of the superficial. Before that first retreat I had no idea how healing and re-energizing silence could be. I return to Grand Coteau every autumn to enjoy the most complete sense of peace I have ever known. When I am at Our Lady of the Oaks I feel as though I have come home.

I feel the same way while on retreat at the Jesuit Spirituality Center in St. Charles College. I've made several weekend retreats there, as well as having made a Spiritual Exercises retreat. These experiences are refreshing to the spirit and conducive to heartfelt prayer.

Having attended fifteen to twenty retreats in Grand Coteau before beginning to write this book in 2002, I felt I was relatively knowledgeable about the place. However, there is quite a lot I didn't know about the history and mystery of this unusual community. So I dug it out, as best I could over a two and a half year period, with the help of a research assistant and the cooperation of Jesuit priests and brothers, Religious of the Sacred Heart, Sisters of the Holy Family, historians, archivists, and townspeople.

I didn't know, for example, that the Convent of the Sacred Heart had been a trilingual international novitiate for the training of religious sisters who would open or work in Sacred Heart schools in the United States, Latin America and New Zealand. I didn't know that the Jesuit novitiate at St. Charles College was and is the seminary for the training of Jesuit priests and brothers for a ten-state area. I had no idea that John Berchmans, who appeared to Mary Wilson in the famous Miracle of Grand Coteau, wasn't the only saint who spent time at the Academy of the Sacred Heart. I had no knowledge of the fascinating story behind the Thensted Outreach Center, established by Sacred Heart Sister Margaret Hoffman as a means of continuing the charitable work of the legendary Fr. Cornelius Thensted, S.J. Nor was I vaguely aware of the transforming power of the Spiritual Exercises of St. Ignatius, which is the basis for most of the retreats at the Jesuit Spirituality Center and at Our Lady of the Oaks Retreat House.

Having learned these things in the course of researching and interviewing for this book, I now feel I have a better understanding of the character of the community. And I am convinced now, more than ever before, that Grand Coteau is indeed one of the truly holy places in North America.

– Trent Angers

For
Felix "Buck" Martin
and
Brother George Murphy, S.J.,
two of Grand Coteau's
finest citizens,
whose countless prayers
and deeds of kindness
have helped to make
this world a better place
in which to live

Acknowledgements

Researching, interviewing for and writing any book in the non-fiction genre always requires the help and cooperation of quite a few people. I am grateful to the many who helped bring this one to fruition.

Bonnie Taylor Barry worked as my research assistant, poring through the Minister's Diary of St. Charles College and interviewing several Grand Coteau residents to provide a clear picture of the religious and social milieu of the town throughout the twentieth century and even earlier.

Access to critical information was provided by the staff and management of six religious and educational institutions in Grand Coteau, namely Our Lady of the Oaks Retreat House, St. Charles College, the Academy of the Sacred Heart, the Thensted Center, St. Charles Borromeo Church and St. Ignatius School.

Rare documents and old photographs were obtained from three archival collections. Thanks are in order to Fr. Donald Hawkins, S.J., and Joan Gaulene of the Jesuits' archives at Loyola University in New Orleans; to Sr. Fran Gimber, Sr. Mary Louise Gavan and Sr. Margaret Phelan of the Society of the Sacred Heart National Archives in St. Louis; and to Barbara DeJean of the Diocese of Lafayette Archives in Lafayette, La.

Some four dozen people – mostly Sacred Heart sisters, Jesuit priests and brothers, and Grand Coteau townspeople – consented to interviews for the book, thus helping us to better understand the history and the spirituality of Grand Coteau. Their names can be found in the bibliography under "Personal Interviews."

A dozen or more photographers contributed pictures to illustrate much of what is stated in the text. Their names are listed in the photo credits toward the back of the book.

The staff of Acadian House Publishing was engaged with this project for more than two years, and thanks are in order to them: Jon Russo, who designed and produced the book; Cheryl Devillier and Carolyn Estilette, who typed it; Neal Bertrand, who proofread every word (more than once); and Wes Milligan, who reviewed the final manuscript and helped with fact-checking.

– T. A.

Contents

GRAND COTEAU

The Holy Land of South Louisiana

The 1½-mile-long oak alley which links the Academy of the Sacred Heart with St. Charles College was planted in 1837 and is largely intact today. The trees were planted in part to provide shade for the horses of the Jesuit chaplains as they would travel between the Academy and the Jesuit residence. The oak alley literally and symbolically links the Jesuits and the Religious of the Sacred Heart — a connection that has remained strong into the twenty-first century.

Chapter One

The Character of Grand Coteau

NESTLED IN THE HEART OF THE CAJUN COUNTRY OF southern Louisiana is a village called Grand Coteau, an intriguing and somewhat mysterious place with well-established ties to the supernatural. You wouldn't know it at first glance, but this quiet community has played a significant role in the annals of Christianity in North America.

The village is often referred to as a holy place, as sacred ground. It has been sanctified by the celebration of thousands of Masses, by the visitations of saints, by the spectacular Miracle of Grand Coteau, and by a Christian spirit that has inspired countless prayers and works of mercy among the people who have called Grand Coteau their home.

Long known as a center for religious retreats and Catholic education, Grand Coteau is widely recognized as the home of the Academy of the Sacred Heart, Our Lady of the Oaks Retreat House, and St. Charles College, which serves as a Jesuit seminary and spirituality center.

An aura of mystery is always in the air in this historic community, because of its unusual architecture, its ancient and intriguing cemeteries, its abundance of hauntingly beautiful moss-draped oaks, and its rich religious heritage. Adding to the mystique are the stories that circulate about the deeds of holy men and women who have lived here and about the saints who have come quietly to visit this special place.

Grand Coteau, which is French for "Big Ridge," is situated on high ground compared with much of the land around it. It is located adjacent to Interstate 49,

Founded in 1819 to serve the people of the Grand Coteau area, St. Charles Borromeo Church is noted for its rare architecture and beautiful artwork. **Above:** The church is located in front of a cemetery for Jesuit priests and brothers. **Right:** A "Pietà" is among the beautiful statues in the church. **Facing page:** One of the tall stained glass windows depicts the washing of the feet of Jesus.

between the cities of Lafayette and Opelousas, about 150 miles west of New Orleans. The first known inhabitants of the area were Native American Indians of the Attakapas Tribe. The issuing of Spanish land grants in 1776 brought Anglo-American and Irish farmers, who were followed by German and French settlers, then African slaves and Acadian exiles. With the dawn of the twenty-first century, Grand Coteau was a predominantly black community of 1,100 people and a local government led by black elected officials.

One of the distinguishing characteristics of Grand Coteau is that it doesn't look like any other place. On the main street is St. Charles College, a huge old four-story building that practically begs to be explored. The college and its outbuildings, some of them more than a century old, sit upon a well-kept and expansive lawn that is surely one of the biggest yards in the South. Behind the college is St. Charles Borromeo Church, which features a distinctive, much-photographed Second Empire-style belfry with a 3,000-pound bell that peals at noon each day and can be heard by everyone in town. A stone's throw away is Our Lady of the Oaks Retreat House, a comfortable, inviting facility built in a Spanish architectural style and enclosing a shaded courtyard. The driveway leading to

the building is lined with beautiful old oaks and Stations of the Cross. About a mile down the road is the Academy of the Sacred Heart, whose oldest building — a four-story, red brick convent-school — looks very much as it did prior to the Civil War. On the second floor is the Shrine of St. John Berchmans, who was instrumental in the famous miracle of 1866; the shrine is located in the same room where the miracle occurred.

Another characteristic of Grand Coteau is its peace and tranquility. Nobody ever seems to be in a hurry here — not the retreatants milling about the grounds in prayer and reflection, nor the ladies browsing in the shops across the highway from the college, nor the townspeople strolling home from morning Mass. People here move at a natural pace, a human pace.

The cemeteries of Grand Coteau bear witness to the longevity of the community; the headstones illuminate the history of a nation and speak words of love for the deceased and words of hope for their eternal reward.

Some local citizens have observed that there are more people dead than alive in Grand Coteau, more laid out in the graveyards than walking around town. This is true, and there is good reason why it is so: The cemeteries have been collecting the bodies of the deceased for a very long time, since the late 1700s. Still, for a town of only 1,100 living people, the cemeteries seem extensive.

In all, there are four cemeteries in town. The largest is Grand Coteau's community graveyard, called St. Charles Cemetery. It is located behind Our Lady of the Oaks Retreat House and contains graves dating back to the late 1700s, many of which are painted every year or two on All Saints' Day by survivors of the deceased. Adjacent to this graveyard is the old Jesuit Cemetery, which holds the mortal remains of Jesuit priests and brothers and dates to the mid-1800s. The new Jesuit Cemetery, on the south side of Our Lady of the Oaks, picks up where the old one left off, starting with a headstone marked 1885. Among the notable graves in this plot are those of two Jesuits, buried side by side, whose relatives played major but opposing roles in the Civil War. One is Fr. Thomas Sherman (1856-1933), the son of Union General William Tecumseh Sherman, while the other is Fr. John Salter (1877-1933), the grandnephew of Alexander Stephens, Vice President of the Confederacy. The Sacred Heart Cemetery, located behind the Academy, contains the remains of members of the Society of the Sacred Heart, including Mary Wilson, who was cured in the Miracle of Grand Coteau.

Jesuit novices make their vows of poverty, chastity and obedience during a special Vow Mass at St. Charles Borromeo Church in August of 2004. Receiving the vows is Jesuit Provincial Fr. Fred Kammer. The church was filled to overflowing, and the Mass was concelebrated by more than 30 priests.

The people of Grand Coteau

Widely known as a center for religious retreats and Catholic education, Grand Coteau is a peaceful and tranquil place, where people seldom seem to be in a hurry.

Fr. Frank Coco, S.J., stationed at Our Lady of the Oaks Retreat House, is a jazz clarinetist who occasionally entertains retreatants with inspirational tunes. He has played with famous musicians such as Al Hirt and Pete Fountain.

Felix "Buck" Martin (1912-2004) was a man of prayer, a pillar of the community, and one of the friendliest people in town. In his younger day he attended the school for black children on the grounds of the Academy of the Sacred Heart.

Sometime in the 1980s a Jesuit priest was giving a homily, talking to a group of visitors who previously had been asking questions about the character of Grand Coteau. Where do the local people work? Are there any large businesses here? What is the main industry?

"The main industry in Grand Coteau is religion," the priest stated respectfully.

While it may not be accurate to refer to religion as an industry, it is true that the teaching and learning of religion and the worship of God are, in one form or another, among the main activities occurring daily in this town.

The primary religious institutions of Grand Coteau — the ones that are known nationally and internationally — are the Academy of the Sacred Heart, St. Charles College and Our Lady of the Oaks Retreat House. Others that are less widely known, but nonetheless very important in the life of the community, are St. Charles Borromeo Church, St. Ignatius School and the Thensted Outreach Center.

The **Academy of the Sacred Heart**, established in 1821, is one of the oldest educational institutions in the United States west of the Mississippi River. Founded by the Society of the Sacred Heart of Jesus, it is part of an international network of

Academy of the Sacred Heart students Nikki Vidos (left) and Marcelle Leger enjoy a light moment with Marcelle's pet, "Tibet," following the annual blessing of the animals, held on the feast of St. Francis of Assisi.

Julia Eaglin Key, a teacher for 37 years, was educated by Jesuits and Sacred Heart sisters while growing up in Grand Coteau. Her parents imbued her and her siblings with the idea that a good education is the means to a better life.

212 such schools and has the distinction of being in continuous operation longer than every other Sacred Heart school in the world. In addition to being a top-flight, all-girls Catholic school, the Academy was once a trilingual international novitiate, training religious sisters to open and/or to work in Sacred Heart schools throughout the Western Hemisphere.

Some sixteen years after the arrival of the Sacred Heart sisters in Grand Coteau, the Jesuits came and built **St. Charles College**. It functioned as an all-boys Catholic school from 1838 to 1922. In 1922 the college became a Jesuit novitiate, or seminary, a role in which it continues today. In 1972 the college also began operating as the Jesuit Spirituality Center, a retreat house. The primary mission of the retreat house is the giving and making of the Spiritual Exercises of St. Ignatius Loyola, a form of contemplative prayer designed to strengthen the retreatants' spiritual lives and to bring them into a deeper relationship with God.

Coinciding with the one hundredth anniversary of the opening of St. Charles College, **Our Lady of the Oaks Retreat House** was opened in 1938 to augment the retreats being given at the college. The retreats at both houses are based on the Spiritual Exercises, those at the college being one-on-one directed retreats and

Willie Barry grew up in the 1920s and '30s directly across the street from St. Charles College, which functioned solely as a Jesuit novitiate at the time. He still has fond memories of many adventures at the college, from playing sandlot football and baseball to learning photography from the Jesuits.

Jesuit novice Bao Nguyen and Marianite Sister Audrey Fontenot enjoy a light moment at an Opelousas, La., nursing home. Novices make regular apostolic visits as part of their novitiate training.

those at Our Lady of the Oaks taking the form of preached, or conference, retreats.

Next door to Our Lady of the Oaks is the **Church of St. Charles Borromeo**, founded by the Vincentian Order in 1819 to serve the people of the Grand Coteau area. The Jesuits took over the church's operations in 1837 and have been at the helm ever since. The existing church building was constructed in 1879-80, and its name was changed to Sacred Heart Church at that time; it was changed back to its original name in 1971.

Listed on the National Register of Historic Places, the church is noted for its rare architecture and exceptionally beautiful stained glass windows, oil paintings and statues.

The church was named for a sixteenth century Bishop of Milan, Italy. St. Charles Borromeo (1538-1584) was a noted church reformer who was most active at a time when the church was mired in scandal among the clergy and laity. Through his urgings, and especially by his example, he brought many disillusioned Catholics back into the church after they had left because of the corruption and scandals. Sometimes referred to as "Father of the Clergy," he led an exemplary life of prayer,

Pre-kindergarten teacher Yvonne Sonnier works with her student, Angele Pellerin, during class at St. Ignatius School. Founded in 1890 by the Religious of the Sacred Heart, the school is now run by lay educators.

Robert Frugé, who offers carriage rides through Grand Coteau on weekends, is an attorney and owner of a local bed-and-breakfast inn. Like the pace of the community in general, the carriage rides are never rushed.

works of charity, integrity and church leadership.

The Church of St. Charles Borromeo is the parish church of Grand Coteau and the surrounding area, providing regular Masses and offering the sacraments to parishioners and the children of St. Ignatius School, which is located on the grounds adjacent to the church.

St. Charles Chapel (originally called Christ the King Church) was built by the black community a few doors down from St. Charles Borromeo Church. It functioned as a separate church for blacks from 1942 to 1971, when Grand Coteau's two congregations were united into one. The chapel features a regular Sunday Mass, plus Masses on special occasions.

St. Ignatius School, which provides a traditional Catholic education to boys and girls from pre-kindergarten through eighth grade, has been in operation since 1890. Founded by the Religious of the Sacred Heart, the school was under their administration from 1890 to 1950 and again from 1975 to 1985. The Sisters of St. Joseph ran the school from 1950 to 1975. Lay educators took over in 1985. The school was originally called Sacred Heart Parochial, but changed to St. Ignatius School in 1956, in honor of St. Ignatius Loyola, founder of the Jesuit order and patron

For a town of only 1,100 residents, Grand Coteau seems to have more than its share of cemeteries: two for Jesuits, one for Religious of the Sacred Heart, and one for the community in general. The large number of graves is a reflection of the age of the community, which was begun in the eighteenth century. **Above:** The community graveyard, known as St. Charles Cemetery, includes numerous age-worn graves going back to the 1700s. **Right:** Betty Broussard of Grand Coteau paints the grave of her husband on All Saints' Day, 2002.

saint of schools.

In addition to its affiliation with St. Ignatius School, St. Charles Borromeo Church supports the **Thensted Outreach Center**, which serves the economically disadvantaged of Grand Coteau and the surrounding area. The center's programs include summertime activities and after-school tutoring for children; food, clothing and visits for elderly shut-ins; and counseling on family and financial matters for whoever needs it.

The center was started in 1982 by Sacred Heart Sister Margaret "Mike" Hoffman as a means of continuing the

Grand Coteau

Way down in Louisiana
Where the oaks and green moss grow
There's a friendly little village
by the name of Grand Coteau.

It's a perfect little Eden
nestled in among the pines;
Where honeysuckle bushes
cluster round the holy shrines.

It's a place of happy living –
Where peace and love prevail,
No troubles, woes nor worries
upon your soul impale –

I love Louisiana
and its town called Grand Coteau –
I'd love to live forever in the
magic of its glow.

– Michael Brahma

This poem, said to have been written in the mid-1800s, was located in the attic of a Grand Coteau residence in the 1970s.

charitable work done by Fr. Cornelius Thensted, S.J. A rugged, determined, saintly man, Fr. Thensted worked for more than a quarter of a century in the Grand Coteau area. He was completely devoted to improving the spiritual, educational and economic lot of the black community, a task at which he succeeded in great measure.

The Thensted Center occupies the building once used by St. Peter Claver High School (1947 to 1977), a school for blacks built under the direction of Fr. Thensted and staffed by the Sisters of the Holy Family. Next to this building is the former St. Peter Claver Elementary, now called Grand Coteau Elementary, founded by the Sacred Heart sisters. This school, originally called Sacred Heart Colored School, was formally established in 1875 on the grounds of the Academy of the Sacred Heart.

When they established the school, the sisters were well aware of Southern society's prejudice against the education of blacks; however, the sisters viewed blacks as children of God, in need of an education to equip them to function in the new world which was unfolding following the War Between the States. The sisters' perception of things, their worldview, was guided not by civil law or the societal norms and conventions of the day, but by a much higher law: Jesus' gentle but powerful

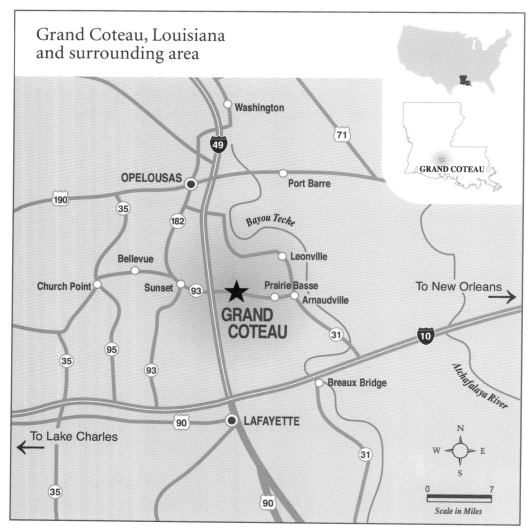

Grand Coteau, Louisiana
and surrounding area

command to love one another. His word was their mantra: "As often as you did it for one of my least brothers, you did it for me."

Like the Jesuit priests and brothers, the Sacred Heart sisters have been guided always by this commandment, this essential Christian spirit, even before their arrival in Grand Coteau in 1821. The Religious of the Sacred Heart and the Jesuits came to teach, and they continue to teach today — in the Academy, in the Thensted Center, from the pulpit, in the retreat houses. For decades and decades, true to their calling, they have consistently delivered the timeless messages of the Gospels, and in doing so have contributed greatly to Grand Coteau's reputation as a truly holy place.

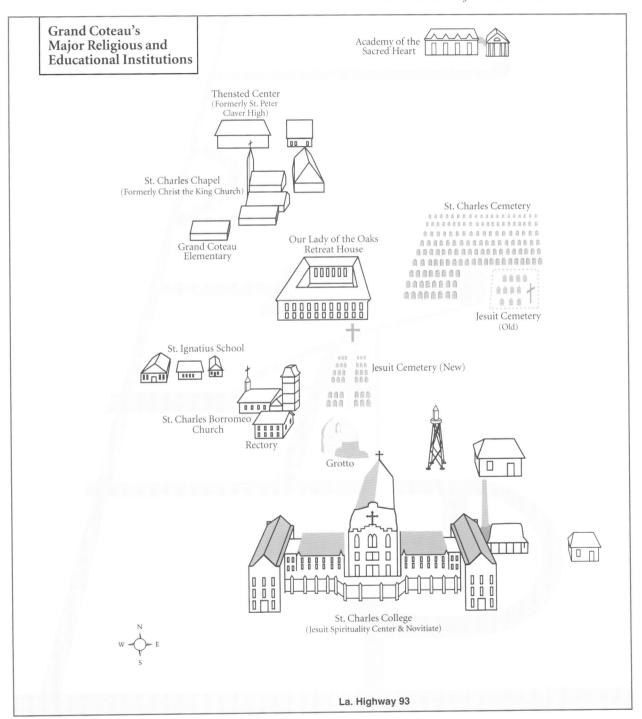

Grand Coteau's Major Religious and Educational Institutions

Academy of the Sacred Heart

Thensted Center
(Formerly St. Peter Claver High)

St. Charles Chapel
(Formerly Christ the King Church)

Grand Coteau Elementary

Our Lady of the Oaks Retreat House

St. Charles Cemetery

Jesuit Cemetery
(Old)

St. Ignatius School

Jesuit Cemetery (New)

St. Charles Borromeo Church

Rectory

Grotto

St. Charles College
(Jesuit Spirituality Center & Novitiate)

N
W E
S

La. Highway 93

The Academy of the Sacred Heart is an all-girls Catholic school founded by the Religious of the Sacred Heart in 1821. One of 212 such institutions around the world, it has been in continuous operation longer than any other.

Chapter Two

Academy of the Sacred Heart

Located in a rural setting on the outskirts of historic Grand Coteau, the Academy of the Sacred Heart is nearing completion of its second century of continuous operation as an all-girls Catholic school. Founded in 1821, it has the distinction of being one of the oldest educational institutions west of the Mississippi River.

While those with a keen eye for history may marvel at the sheer age of the Academy, at its ability to survive for so long, others recognize its most outstanding characteristic as its resounding success in its mission to educate young women.

The Academy was founded by the Religious of the Sacred Heart, an order of nuns established in France in 1800 by Mother Madeleine Sophie Barat, who was declared a saint by the Catholic Church in 1925. The Academy is part of a worldwide network of 212 Sacred Heart schools, all of which have the same mission. The school at Grand Coteau has been in continuous operation longer that any other Sacred Heart school in the world. In addition to educating girls in elementary grades and high school – and even college for a number of years – the Academy once served as an international novitiate for the training of nuns who opened or worked in Sacred Heart schools in North America, South America and New Zealand.

Naturally, the Academy's storied history is marked by the ebbs and flows of fortune. It has enjoyed times of considerable prosperity and suffered through periods of grinding poverty. It lost some of its much-needed nuns to yellow fever during the late 1800s, but remained high and dry and free of cholera during the

The Academy of the Sacred Heart features rich traditions and beautiful surroundings.
Facing page: *The front yard of the Academy has a formal French garden encircling a statue of Jesus baring his Sacred Heart. Beyond the statue is the oak alley, planted in 1837, which connects the Academy with St. Charles College.* **Above:** *The Academy's graduating class of 2004, the 182nd such class, processes to commencement exercises, which take place under the ancient oaks across the street from the main building.*

Great Flood of 1927. It managed to escape the destruction of the Civil War, but suffered greatly through the economic depression and turmoil of the Reconstruction Era. And through it all, the dedicated Religious of the Sacred Heart went quietly and prayerfully about the business of turning out some of the best-educated young women the nation has ever seen.

A few years after its deliverance from potential catastrophe during the Civil War, the Academy was graced by the occurrence of the first authenticated miracle in North America. In the winter of 1866, in what came to be known simply as The Miracle of Grand Coteau, a young postulant named Mary Wilson was instantaneously and totally cured of a severe and life-threatening illness as her fellow nuns made a novena to Blessed John Berchmans.

This supernatural occurrence within the walls of the Academy has led many to the idea that this is a truly sacred place. It is also considered to be sacred because of what has gone on here for so many years, day in and day out, as a place of prayer and worship, as a convent, as a novitiate for the training of the Religious of the Sacred Heart, and as a school dedicated, ultimately, to the spreading of the Gospel of Jesus Christ.

Religious of the Sacred Heart who staffed the Thensted Outreach Center in the early 1990s take time out for a picture. Left to right are Sr. Theresa Downey, Sr. Georgeann Parizek, Sr. Alice Mills, Sr. Nancy Bremner and Sr. Margaret "Mike" Hoffman (founder of the center). While some of the sisters who reside in Grand Coteau today work in the traditional role of teacher at the Academy of the Sacred Heart, others, including those shown here, have been engaged in various ministries of service to the poor and disadvantaged. Their work at the Thensted Center has included tutoring, counseling, visiting the sick and homebound, and organizing gatherings for the elderly. Another ministry of the Religious of the Sacred Heart, located in nearby Opelousas, is the New Life Center, a shelter for homeless women and children.

An enduring commitment to a well-rounded education

For the better part of two centuries, the mission of the Sacred Heart Schools has been simple and well-focused: to prepare young women to become faith-filled, self-confident and effective leaders of tomorrow. The school's intention is "to educate the whole child," to develop her intellectual, physical, emotional and spiritual potential.

Toward these ends, the leaders of the Society of the Sacred Heart, on several occasions down through history, have issued statements defining the essence of a Sacred Heart education and the principles and techniques involved in achieving it.

An updated version of this statement, issued in 1975 and sharpened further in 1990, is required reading not only for the teachers but also for the entire student body and their parents. It is titled *Goals and Criteria for Sacred Heart Schools in the United States*. The document points out that all Sacred Heart Schools are committed to educating their students to the following:

1. A personal and active faith in God.
2. A deep respect for intellectual values.
3. A social awareness which impels to action.
4. The building of community as a Christian value.
5. Personal growth in an atmosphere of wise freedom.

The introduction to the *Goals and Criteria* notes:

> The 1990 Goals and Criteria express the values, the intentions, and the hopes of the Sacred Heart tradition, sharpened to meet the needs of a rapidly changing world....The challenge...continues to lie in the five elements that have been the framework of Sacred Heart education since its beginning, in 1800. These principles are ageless.

The school's approach to teaching these principles is not only academic and theoretical but practical and applied. This helps to ensure that these key lessons will be internalized, taken to heart, and therefore, hopefully, never to be lost as the girls venture forth into the world after graduation. They have, in effect, completed a course in what could be called applied Christianity, and have some practice at walking the walk of persons who are Christian in name and in deed.

This is certainly true with the Third Goal, teaching "a social awareness which impels to action." Each student who graduates puts in a certain number of community-service hours by performing spiritual and corporal works of mercy toward the less fortunate of society. These activities include serving food to the poor at St. Joseph's Diner in nearby Lafayette, collecting shoes for needy children in Mexico, painting and repairing the homes of the elderly in the Grand Coteau area, and mentoring and tutoring pupils of nearby Sunset Elementary School.

Many of the older girls participate in projects set up by the worldwide Network of Sacred Heart Schools. For instance, some go to New York for a month or more in the summer to serve the homeless, while others go to the St. Madeleine Sophie Center in San Diego, California, to work with mentally handicapped adults.

The junior class studies the Church's encyclicals on social justice issues in an effort to connect the Church's teachings with the world in which they live.

A brief history of the Academy of the Sacred Heart

Founded in 1821 as the Institute for the Education of Young Ladies, the Academy of the Sacred Heart at Grand Coteau has established itself as one of the oldest educational institutions west of the Mississippi River.

Even during the War Between the States, when other Southern schools were forced to close due to lack of resources of every kind, this Academy remained open, by the grace of God and with the assistance of a most unlikely benefactor. As a result, its administrators of today are able to boast that of all the 212 Sacred Heart schools in the world, the Academy at Grand Coteau has been in continuous operation longer than any other.

The school has its roots in the generosity of Mrs. Charles Smith, the wealthy widow of a south Louisiana planter, who donated the land and the first buildings to the Society of the Sacred Heart. In addition to the real estate, she provided a few slaves to work the land and paid for transportation for two nuns to travel from St. Louis to Grand Coteau to open the school.

Mother Philippine Duchesne, who brought the Society of the Sacred Heart from France to America in 1818, sent two members of the Society from Missouri to south Louisiana to start the school. Mother Eugénie Audé and Sister Mary Layton left St. Louis on August 5, 1821, and arrived in Grand Coteau three weeks later.

The arduous journey began aboard the steamboat *La Rapide*, which took them down the Mississippi River to Plaquemine, Louisiana. From there they traveled westward on ox cart, flatboat and horseback in the sweltering heat, humidity, rain and mud.

The travel-weary religious with sunburned faces and soiled habits were greeted by Mrs. Smith, who fed and cared for them in her own home for three weeks before they took up residence in the house that would also serve as the school.

The building was fifty-five feet square, two-storied, surrounded by a veranda,

The original house that was the Academy of the Sacred Heart served as both a school and a convent. The house and the large tract of land upon which it was located were gifts from Mrs. Charles Smith.

and had a dirt floor. There were two other small buildings, one of which served as a kitchen and the other a dining room. The buildings were situated near the middle of a 150-acre farm that produced cotton and sugarcane and that featured an orchard of fig and peach trees.

While the two nuns were most grateful for Mrs. Smith's generous gift, this rustic place was a far cry from the accommodations to which they were accustomed, to put it mildly. Not only were the floors merely dirt, but there was no furniture in the building; not only were there no locks for the doors, but the cracks in the doors and windows were wide enough to let in droves of mosquitoes and every manner of feathered and scaly creature.

Despite these and other adversities, the two religious labored diligently and opened their school to five students in October, less than two months after their arrival.

For the first three months Mother Audé was the Academy's only teacher. Some six months later, in April of 1822, she was joined by Mother Anna Xavier Murphy, who had come from France and who was destined to play a major role in guiding

The staff and faculty of the Academy of the Sacred Heart at Grand Coteau gather for a portrait in 1946. The traditional black and white habit has been replaced by more informal attire.

the Academy through the challenges of the next fourteen years. Accompanying Mother Murphy were several postulants, including Carmelite Landry from the Bayou Lafourche area of southern Louisiana.

The religious worked through setbacks of various kinds and, with the continuing financial assistance of Mrs. Smith, managed to establish their humble school and convent in relatively good fashion in less than a year.

Mother Duchesne visited the fledgling school one year after its opening and was gratified to see the degree of progress made in such a short time. She reported to her superior, Reverend Mother Sophie Barat, the founder of the order:

> Our house at Opelousas is, at the end of its first year, well-organized and completely free from debt. The chapel is pretty and devotional, the sacristy well supplied with sacred vessels, thanks to the generosity of several priests. The academy has seventeen pupils, and five or six others are expected immediately. They are making remarkable progress in piety and in their studies....

Mother Duchesne visited Grand Coteau again in 1829, again making the three-week journey from St. Louis. Once more she expressed satisfaction with the progress of the school, which was now under the direction of Mother Murphy.

The 1830s was a time of growth and stability for the Catholic institution. By 1835 the student body exceeded one hundred girls, and the community of nuns stood at twelve. It was also a time of relative prosperity. The farming operation and the Academy itself were profitable to the point that the nuns were able to send fair sums of money northward to the less prosperous Missouri Sacred Heart communities at St. Louis and Florissant. Some of the money was used to support orphans in St. Louis.

The 1830s was a dreadful time in much of the Deep South as yellow fever ravaged the land and sent young and old, slave and free person, to their graves. The religious of the Sacred Heart prayed fervently and frequently that they and their students and their slaves would be spared from this often-fatal disease. And they were spared, for the most part, though in 1836 the fever claimed the lives of Mother Murphy and her nurse, Mother Rose Elder.

Another burden the nuns bore, with impatience, was the absence of a priest to celebrate Mass and to administer the sacraments on a regular basis. While various priests did spend time at the Academy as their schedules permitted, the nuns would sometimes go for months without even seeing a priest. Residing as they did in such a remote area, the nuns had to live with a shortage of priests, as did the Catholic laity in the sparsely populated climes of central and northern Louisiana.

In a letter written to Bishop Joseph Rosati, Bishop of St. Louis, in November of 1832, Mother Murphy makes one of several requests for priests, particularly Jesuits, to be permanently stationed at Grand Coteau.

"We...bemoan the poverty of our Diocese in regard to talented clergymen. You ought to share with us...the sons of Loyola...," she writes.

Four months later, in February of 1833, she writes the Bishop again:

"We want a college here. See what can be done."

In 1837 the leadership of the Academy was assumed by Mother Julie Bazire. Taking up where Mother Murphy left off, Mother Bazire continued writing the Bishop and having her community pray that the Jesuits would one day come and settle in Grand Coteau.

A major enticement – free land, and lots of it – was dangled in front of the Bishop and the Jesuit superior by the determined Mother Bazire. She pointed out on several occasions the availability of the beautiful tract of land, adjacent to land owned by her religious order, which Mrs. Smith had set aside for the furtherance of Catholic education.

The problem was, however, the Jesuits were seriously considering opening a college in Donaldsonville, between New Orleans and Baton Rouge, and the deal appeared to be all but sealed. But the plan stalled due to opposition from some influential citizens of Donaldsonville.

It was during this brief delay, this fleeting moment of opportunity, that the

Since the 1830s Jesuit priests have helped meet the spiritual needs of students and faculty at the Academy of the Sacred Heart, saying Masses, hearing confessions, and giving retreats. **Above:** Fr. James Chamard, S.J., poses with Academy students in 1935. **Below:** Fr. Auguste Coyle, S.J., poses with graduating seniors in 1960.

ever-watchful Mother Bazire stepped up and offered a deal sweetened with the *lagniappe* of southern Louisiana. If the Jesuits would come and settle in Grand Coteau, she stated, they would not only receive one hundred acres of land free of charge, but the nuns would throw in 200,000 bricks to help build the Jesuits' college! She had the Jesuit superior's undivided attention, and he could clearly see in his mind's eye not only a huge and valuable piece of land but also a shiny new brick college sitting upon it. (The bricks, by the way, had been made in the nuns' brickyard for a chapel they planned to build.)

It was an offer the level-headed Jesuits could not refuse. They accepted, and construction of the first Jesuit college in the South was begun in the summer of 1837. The nuns' crusade to attract the Jesuits to Grand Coteau had been won by prayer, logic, free land, several tons of homemade bricks, and a keen sense of timing by a woman of determination.

Literally and symbolically linking the Academy of the Sacred Heart and the new Jesuit college, Fr. Nicholas Point, S.J., planted a one-and-a-half-mile alley of oaks from the front of the Academy to the construction site of the new college. Fr. Point, the first rector of what would be named St. Charles College, planted the trees the same year that work began on the college. The oak alley, which came to be known as Oakdale, is largely intact today. The oaks were planted in part to provide shade for the horses of the Jesuit chaplains as they would travel between the Academy and the Jesuits' residence.

In 1851, fourteen years after giving away all their bricks to the Jesuits, the nuns completed their new brick chapel adjacent to the Academy's main building.

Times were good for the Religious of the Sacred Heart at Grand Coteau as they entered the 1860s. Four decades had passed since they opened their school. They were succeeding nicely in their mission to provide top-flight Catholic education to girls and to spread the Good News about the Lord whom they served.

Civil War comes to Grand Coteau

In the forty years the Religious of the Sacred Heart had been in Grand Coteau they had had their share of life's burdens, enduring the rigors of establishing a convent in the middle of nowhere, trying to dodge recurring epidemics of yellow fever, and living with the ever-present financial stresses of a growing educational institution.

But now, entering the decade of the 1860s, the nuns were confronted with a new source of anxiety as the talk of war between the states grew louder and more angry in both the North and the South. Several of the Southern states were considering seceding from the Union over the issues of slavery and states' rights. The United States government was threatening war, if necessary, to force the Southern states to remain part of the Union.

Apprehension and uncertainty were the order of the day throughout Louisiana and much of the South. The nuns didn't know what to expect, nor did the towns-people of Grand Coteau, nor the Jesuits of St. Charles College, nor the parents of the children being cared for at the Academy of the Sacred Heart. The anxiety of not knowing was sometimes intense. The thought of the Academy being forced to close was a real concern. So was the fear of the Academy being destroyed by Union forces to prevent it from falling into the hands of the Confederates. The thought of starving to death also crossed the minds of the otherwise hopeful nuns.

Despite the efforts of many in the North and the South to work out their seemingly irreconcilable differences through non-violent means, the war started on April 12, 1861, with the battle of Fort Sumter, South Carolina.

The nuns spent many an hour on their knees in prayer, petitioning the Lord that they might be spared the destruction of war. They were keenly aware of the fact that the Academy they and their predecessors had built over forty years could be obliterated in a matter of hours. Prayers for mercy and deliverance filled their beautiful little chapel, as news of all-out war trickled in to their peaceful community.

A glimmer of hope, a promising bit of news, was received by Mother Amélie Jouve, who was in charge of the Academy at the time, when she learned that one of the Union generals who was leading his troops into the South was the father of a girl in another Sacred Heart school, in Manhattanville, New York. Surely Gen. Nathaniel Banks would not allow harm to come to a school operated by the same order of nuns as those teaching his daughter.

Armed with this logic and hope, Mother Jouve wrote to the head of the school at Manhattanville – who happened to be none other than Mother Aloysia Hardey, a former student and novice of the Academy of the Sacred Heart at Grand Coteau. In turn, Mother Hardey promptly contacted Gen. Banks' wife, asking her to write to her husband and request that he look after the nuns and students and spare the Academy from any harm. Mrs. Banks did write to her husband, and Gen. Banks did agree to honor her request.

In the first months of 1863, Gen. Banks and his 30,000 troops poured into the Teche Country of southern Louisiana, then made their way through the

The Battle of Grand Coteau, also known as the Battle of Bayou Bourbeaux, took place on November 3, 1863. Parts of the battlefield action were witnessed by some of the Sacred Heart sisters, watching from the second floor balcony of the Academy. This sketch, which is said to depict a "furious Rebel attack on the 60th Indiana," was done by C.E.H. Bonwili and appeared in Frank Leslie's Illustrated Newspaper on December 12, 1863.

Attakapas District to Grand Coteau. They settled in the fields around Grand Coteau and Sunset for a few weeks, occupying the area and taking on the Confederates in several minor battles. The Federal forces took Opelousas, a major community just north of Grand Coteau, on April 20.

True to his word, Gen. Banks saw to it that no harm came to the Academy at Grand Coteau. Not only did he spare the school, but he issued orders that it be guarded and protected. And he provided the nuns with a generous amount of food to help them through the war.

Gen. Banks' protective order was written on May 4:

> Officers and soldiers will protect the property and persons of the Convent and College at Grand Coteau. The violation of this safeguard will be punished with death.

Some of the age-worn structures on the campus of the Academy of the Sacred Heart bear witness to the longevity of this venerable institution. **Above:** *The old brick stable, still in use today, dates to the 1880s and is listed on the National Register of Historic Places.*
Facing page: *The old cistern behind the main building was, in days gone by, a primary source of potable water.*

Gen. Banks had his commissary officer supply the convent with one hundred pounds of coffee, five barrels of meal, two barrels of flour, half a chest of tea, one barrel of sugar, and five bags of salt. Later, he added a keg of butter and "a bolt of black merino" (fine wool).

Seeing Gen. Banks' kind and generous spirit – at least toward her school and convent – Mother Jouve thanked him for the food and the protection. In the same breath, she asked that he favor the Sacred Heart convent in Natchitoches with the same treatment. He did as she requested.

The provisions and protection afforded the Academy enabled it to remain open through the war. It had come close to having to suspend operations due to lack of food.

When Gen. Banks and his men left Grand Coteau the area reverted to the control of Confederate rule – "which was no rule at all," according to Fr. C.M. Widman, S.J., who was stationed at St. Charles College at the time. He reported that the soldiers were without proper clothing, shoes or ammunition, and that many deserted and hid in the woods and swamps, living on wild game and fish.

On November 1, 1863, the people of Grand Coteau could hear bugles and drums as a Federal battalion coming from the Teche Country marched through the village. Again, the Federal soldiers camped in the fields on the outskirts of Grand Coteau. As before, the Confederate soldiers used guerrilla tactics, sniping at the Federal troops, then disappearing into the woods before they could be engaged by the opposition.

On the morning of November 3, 1863, the Rebels inflicted 154 casualties on the Yankees in what came to be called the Battle of Bayou Bourbeaux, or the Battle of Grand Coteau. Some 400 Rebels had been hiding in the woods near the town. As 5,000 Yankee soldiers marched from their campsite, the Rebels opened fire with cannons, then muskets. The Union soldiers retreated in disarray, thinking the enemy force to be much stronger than it actually was.

Some of the carnage was witnessed by the nuns from the second-floor balcony of the Academy. They could see men being killed on the road in front of their building and in the tall grass of the nearby fields. Despite the cannon fire and bullets flying in all directions, no one and nothing on the Academy grounds was injured.

The end of the war, in the summer of 1865, did not bring an end to the misery

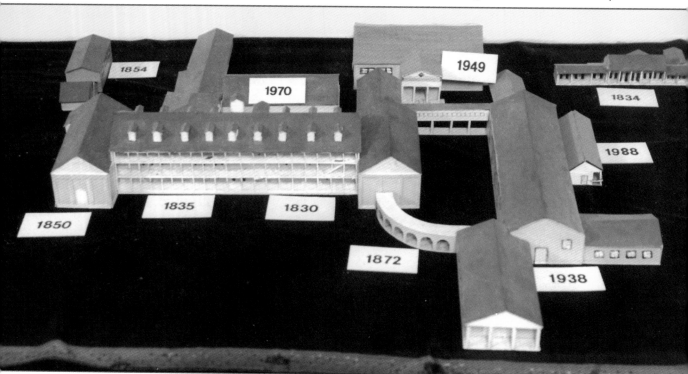

A museum designed to preserve key elements of the history of the Academy is located on the second floor of the main building. Opened in 1993, it contains old letters, documents, photographs, furniture and various other displays. **Above:** *A model of the Academy's buildings, and the dates of their construction, demonstrates how the institution has expanded over the years.* **Facing page:** *A mannequin displays the traditional habit worn in the past by the Religious of the Sacred Heart.*

suffered by virtually everyone in the Grand Coteau area and most of the South. Plantations and farms were devastated, food supplies depleted, Confederate currency worthless, and many of the men who had fought for Southern independence came home physically or emotionally crippled – if they came home at all. In many cases, women and children were left to run the farms as best they could.

With the Emancipation Proclamation having gone into effect on January 1, 1863, many former slaves left the plantations of Louisiana and headed for the cities to search out a better life for themselves and their children. But without much of an education or marketable skills other than farming and cooking, a huge percentage found themselves living a new nightmare, only in a different locale. It was the worst of times for the vast majority of people living in the South.

Toward the end of the war the nuns of the Academy called a meeting with the former slaves who worked their farm. They made it clear that the workers were free to go or to stay. It was their choice. If they stayed, they could continue to work the land and provide labor in the house – in exchange for food, shelter and education. The nuns explained they themselves were virtually penniless and could not pay them with money.

The workers all decided to stay on and to continue doing their jobs. They understood that the education being offered by the nuns would free them even further by equipping them to function in a world with which they were unfamiliar. And if they were not ready to leave before they grew old, then perhaps their children could be prepared, with their help and with the assistance of the nuns, to move off the farm and into a better life.

Educating black people was nothing new for the Sacred Heart nuns. For many years they had provided the slaves with religious training and the rudiments of secular education, such as lessons in reading and writing. Now, with the war having ended, the nuns were acutely aware of how ill-equipped the ex-slaves were to make their own way in the new world. So, they intensified their efforts to educate the former slaves, organizing separate classes for adults and children and spending more time than ever before teaching them.

In 1875 the nuns opened a formal school for black children, called the Sacred Heart Colored School, on the grounds of the Academy, later moving it off campus and into Grand Coteau. The Sacred Heart nuns would run the school for more than seventy years, turning it over to the Jesuits and the Sisters of the Holy Family in 1947.

The school, which eventually became known as St. Peter Claver School, would continue in operation for the better part of the twentieth century.

The years immediately following the Civil War were dismal for the residents of Grand Coteau, as they were for the vast majority of Southerners. The collapse of the economic system and the loss of the war meant anxiety and insecurity over the future. The loss of loved ones in the war meant months or years of sadness and longing that could never be satisfied. It was a time of darkness and despair.

But on December 14, 1866, a glorious event occurred within the walls of the Academy of the Sacred Heart, bringing light and joy to an otherwise despondent population. This supernatural event, known as the Miracle of Grand Coteau, involved the apparition of Blessed John Berchmans and the cure of Mary Wilson, a young woman who was preparing to become a member of the Society of the Sacred Heart. Mary had been suffering from an excruciating and life-threatening illness, and the doctor had given up on her recovery. (See chapter on the miracle, page 53.)

An international novitiate

For much of its history the convent of the Sacred Heart at Grand Coteau served as a novitiate, a training ground for novices who aspired to become full-fledged, permanent members of the Society of the Sacred Heart.

It was an international novitiate for part of the nineteenth century, drawing novices not only from Louisiana and other parts of the United States, but also from Mexico, Cuba and Puerto Rico.

For most of the period from 1821 to 1896, the novitiate was bilingual, with

Mater Admirabilis (Mother Most Admirable) is the title of this painting of the young ➤ Virgin Mary before she became the mother of Jesus. The painting was done in 1844 by a French novice in the Society of the Sacred Heart. This image – in the form of prints, statues and/or etched glass – can be found in all 212 Sacred Heart schools around the world.

Pre-kindergarten students and their mothers enjoy an informal outing under the oaks at the Academy of the Sacred Heart. The traditional event, in which the children honor their moms with song and flowers, is held near Mother's Day each year.

instruction being provided in English and French. It was trilingual from 1874 to 1896, with instruction in Spanish being added for the young women from the Latin American countries.

Like the Academy, the novitiate produced many women of distinction and accomplishment down through the years. Several of them went on to play major roles in the governance of the Society and in the pioneering work of opening new Sacred Heart schools in the U.S. and other countries.

Among the most notable was Mother Aloysia Hardey, from Opelousas, Louisiana, who was a member of the Academy's first class and founder of the Sacred Heart schools at Manhattanville, New York, and other locations. Others of distinction were Mother Suzannah Boudreau, who opened a school in New Zealand, and Mother Mary Elizabeth Moran, who founded schools in Mexico and Puerto Rico.

The work for which these and other nuns were prepared was not for the faint-hearted. In many cases they were pioneers, trailblazers, venturing always into the unknown. Many of them went into foreign countries to carve out a place where they could provide for the Catholic education of young women. Hardships were many, setbacks and misunderstandings were commonplace, and success was not assured. They walked in faith, and their faith bore fruit.

Driven by the Lord's directive to "go out and teach all nations," these missionary nuns approached their work with uncommon zeal and stamina. They were staunchly committed to building the Kingdom of God on earth, and their niche was the formation of girls into strong Catholic women.

When they prayed, "Thy kingdom come, thy will be done, on earth as it is in heaven," they did so not as bystanders who hoped God would make it happen but as participants who felt they were called to spread the Good News of salvation and of God's love for all of humankind.

Like Francis of Assisi and John the Baptist, these women were heralds of the Great King, sent to proclaim the Good News and "to educate strong women for God," as the superior of their order had called upon them to do.

Customs and Traditions

Students attending the Academy today participate in age-old customs and traditions, some of which date back to the mid-1800s. These include *congé*, *goûter*, hiking in the woods, riding horses and wearing school uniforms.

Congé has been celebrated for a century or more. It is a day off, a break from school, given by the school's administrators to celebrate a holiday, a feast day, or a special occasion of some sort. In the old days it could be announced in advance or given spontaneously, sometimes with fanfare. Alumnae who attended the Academy in the 1940s recall being asleep in their dorm rooms and awakened by the older students running up and down the halls shouting "*Congé! Congé!*" and throwing doubloons that could be used to purchase various items from the booths that would be set up for the occasion.

The old-fashioned *congés* included a day of games such as *cache-cache*, a form of hide-and-seek, as well as a formal dinner to cap off the day. Back in the 1930s and '40s three or four *congés* were declared each year; nowadays there are two or three.

The family *congé* today is held in the same holiday spirit, but on a weekend in the spring. It is also an occasion for fund-raising for the school. A typical *congé* features

The Academy of the Sacred Heart has a well-deserved reputation for providing a top-notch education to its students at every grade level. **Above:** *Enjoying time out of the classroom, students Katelyn Green, Meg Francez and Andrée Trahan (left to right) work on a math project using a global positioning device.* **Right:** *Students in the computer lab use modern technology for research, writing and problem-solving.*

food booths, a volleyball tournament and a silent auction, plus the sale of books, craft items, plants and paintings. The parents run the booths and do the cooking.

Through the 1960s the students made a special effort to include orphans in at least one of their *congés* each year. These guests – thirty to forty children – were bused in from St. Mary's Orphanage in Lafayette and treated to a day of fun, including a picnic, softball, volleyball and soccer. This charitable practice continued until the orphanage closed in 1974.

Goûter, or afternoon snack, is another tradition remembered by many of the Academy's alumnae. The girls were served "a little taste of something" such as a muffin, cookies, pecans covered in 'cane syrup, or bread and butter topped with a little sugar.

The Academy is surrounded by countless acres of farmland, pastures and wooded areas. The abundance of open space and fresh air has historically beckoned the girls of the Academy to hike, roam and explore. Some alumnae have fond memories of long hikes in the woods in which they would practically enter into another world, removed from the rigors of the classroom and the study hall, losing track of the time of day and literally forgetting which day of the week it was.

In the 1930s, '40s and '50s, small groups of girls would walk a mile or so into town, into Grand Coteau, just for a change of scenery, and to get a soft drink and candy at one of the community's two grocery stores. Other times they would walk to nearby Sunset to get ice cream at the pharmacy.

The open spaces around the Academy have always been ideal for horseback riding, though much of the riding is done in the fenced-in areas of the school's equestrian center. Here the girls learn to saddle a horse, to ride properly, and to feed and care for the animal.

Historically, the campus culture included being schooled in a regimented fashion, with early bedtimes, fixed study hall hours and mandatory uniforms. In days gone by, when a boy would come to see a girl at the Academy the visits were made in a formal parlor under the watchful eye of one of the nuns.

There were also "politeness classes," in which the girls were taught the proper manner in which a lady should eat, speak, sit, cross her legs and stand. They were taught to stand when an adult entered the room and to curtsy when approaching one of the nuns in charge or passing in front of a statue of the Blessed Virgin Mary. These gestures of respect and courtesy were part and parcel of the education provided by the nuns in this all-girls Catholic school.

The sodalities were student religious organizations that were a significant part of the campus culture for a century or more, until the late 1960s. The kinds of activities and values encouraged by the sodalities included daily Mass, daily meditations and readings, living by the highest moral standards, and keeping Christ at the center of one's life. The Academy sponsored three sodalities, for different age groups. Younger pupils could join the Sodality of St. Aloysius; the Sodality of the Holy Angels was for older students; and the group for the oldest students was known as the Children of Mary. The latter group made commitments to daily Mass and meditation, as well as service within their local church communities.

Alumnae who attended the Academy through the 1960s remember a weekly ceremony called *primes*. The students sat in the auditorium and were called up to the stage one class at a time. The nuns were seated on the stage, with the mother superior in the middle. The girls stood in a semi-circle facing the nuns. When a girl's name was called she would step forward and receive a card that was essentially a conduct grade reflecting her behavior the previous week. The cards were marked "very good," "good" and "fair." Students who had behaved badly didn't receive a card. It was very important to some of the girls what the nuns thought of their behavior; not so important to others. *Primes* was part of the discipline system, though corporal punishment was not involved. Still, the ceremony was stressful to some of the girls. The custom faded away sometime in the 1960s.

Student uniforms have almost always been a standard part of the campus culture. At one time the girls wore brown skirts and white blouses, then navy blue skirts and white blouses, then plaid skirts and white blouses. Brown saddle oxfords were standard dress for many years, as was the black veil for Mass through the 1960s.

One of the enduring traditions of the Academy of the Sacred Heart is prayer before a special statue of the Virgin Mary that goes by the name of *Mater Admirabilis* (Mother Most Admirable). The statue was inspired by a fresco with the same name, painted in Rome in 1844 by Pauline Perdrau, a French novice in the Society of the Sacred Heart.

The original painting is located in the Trinita dei Monti, a convent of the Society of the Sacred Heart in Rome. The image is of a youthful Mary, age fifteen or sixteen, with a pink gown draped with a cream-colored mantle. She bears a calm and peaceful countenance. The painting includes a white lily representing purity of heart, a book symbolizing the value of education, and a spindle which stands for the value of productive work.

The painting got its name from Pope Pius IX. He was visiting the Trinita in 1846 when he saw the fresco for the first time. He found it to be a magnificent piece of art and exclaimed spontaneously, "She is so admirable!" Thus, *Mater Admirabilis*.

A large *Mater* statue is located in the Academy of the Sacred Heart at Grand Coteau, and small ones can be found in various places throughout the school. A copy of the painting hangs on a wall in one of the halls of the Academy.

The *Mater* image – in the form of prints, statues and/or etched glass – can be found in all 212 Sacred Heart schools around the world.

* * * * *

The Academy of the Sacred Heart had its ups and downs through the twentieth century, adding new buildings, growing in student population, and continuing to succeed in its mission to help form strong, well-educated women.

The Academy even broadened its role to include higher education in 1921, giving birth to a two-year Normal College for Teachers. This institution was expanded to a four-year liberal arts college, operating from 1939 through 1956.

In 1996, when the Academy reached its 175th year, the co-editor of the school's annual report, Mona Cravins, wrote an introductory article extolling the school's tradition of educational excellence. The article echoes St. Madeleine Sophie's strongly held belief that the system of Catholic education which she espoused would transform society for the better. Mrs. Cravins, who worked in the Academy's Development Office at the time, stated:

> Having lived and learned, the religious of the Sacred Heart laid a solid foundation for many generations of students. After 175 years, we stand firm on this same foundation, one made by people rich in faith and inspired by the Sacred Heart of Jesus....
>
> We educate students to become pioneer women. We look today for trailblazers: courageous women following the example of our earlier pioneers, who will use our intellectual unrest to educate to new ideas, utilize these new ideas to overcome old problems, [and] challenge social injustices to make truth and community, in their purest form, a reality.... Informed, courageous, generous, Christian women with integrity are needed to help shape our new world.

The faculty and staff of the Academy remain dedicated to preparing such women for the world.

Mary Wilson, a central figure in the Miracle of Grand Coteau, posed for this portrait circa 1865-66, prior to the time she entered the Society of the Sacred Heart.

Chapter Three

THE MIRACLE OF GRAND COTEAU

Not being able to discover any marks of convalescence, but an immediate return to health, from a severe and painful illness, I am unable to explain the transition by any ordinary natural laws.

— Dr. Edward M. Millard, M.D.
February 4, 1867

THE RIVERBOAT RIDE DOWN THE MISSISSIPPI WOULD HAVE been an altogether happy experience for Mary Wilson, but she couldn't get her parents off her mind. They had disowned her for leaving the Presbyterian Church and becoming a Catholic. Her decision to become a nun had sealed their resolution never to see her again.

What sustained this girl of 18 in this time of trial was her belief that her decision to devote her life to the service of God was the right thing to do. She was a person of unusual conviction and determination.

In a portrait of Mary Wilson made shortly before her departure from St. Louis, she has the look of a strong-willed woman. There is a firm and pensive air about her, the look of a person in deep thought, a person detached from the things of the world.

She had this same look as she stood on the deck of the riverboat that was making its way into the Deep South. Mary was headed for St. Michael's Convent, which was situated on the Mississippi River some forty miles west of New Orleans. There she would begin training to become a nun in the Society of the Sacred Heart of Jesus.

Mary Wilson had led a sheltered life before going to St. Louis with her cousin, who had just been married in their hometown, New London, Canada. The girls were so fond of each other that the cousin asked Mary to go along with her on her honeymoon, and Mary readily agreed. It was the summer of 1864, and Mary was 16 years old at the time. Her parents, who had brought her up to be an avid Presbyterian, were uneasy about the trip to St. Louis. This faraway town had a significant French-Catholic population, and, besides, the Civil War was still being fought in the United States. But they had never before denied their daughter anything, and, accordingly, they reluctantly let her go – for two to three weeks, they thought.

While in St. Louis, Mary met and was befriended by several Catholics, including priests, and she found that they were not so much to be feared and disliked as her parents had led her to believe. While in St. Louis, Mary not only became Catholic but also decided to become a nun.

A friend and confidant of Mary's, Father Coghlan, saw the strength of her character and the depth of her convictions and encouraged her to pursue the vocation to which she felt called. It was he who had urged her to enter the convent in southern Louisiana. There, in a milder climate, she might be able to recover her health, which she had been losing since the day her parents disowned her. There, too, she would be out of reach of her parents, who Mary feared might try to take her back to Canada by force.

The riverboat arrived at St. Michael's Convent in June of 1866, and Mary began the first stage of training necessary to become a member of the Society of the Sacred Heart. While Mary was there, Mother Anna Shannon, the superior, observed that she was an excellent candidate for the religious life in all things but one: her health. She had experienced a severe pain in her side on the boat trip to St. Michael's. She was frail, peaked-looking, susceptible to all sorts of illnesses. Her attitude, on the other hand, was perfect. She was humble and prayerful, and she tried to keep smiling while going about her everyday life, even though she didn't feel well. She set a good example for the other postulants.

Mother Shannon conferred with the doctor who attended the sick of St. Michael's, and together they concluded it would be better for Mary to go to the sisters' convent at Grand Coteau since it wasn't as humid there.

It happened that Mother Mary Elizabeth Moran, the second in command at

Grand Coteau, was at the time concluding a visit to St. Michael's and preparing to return to Grand Coteau. Mary was directed to accompany her to Grand Coteau.

The two traveled to New Orleans by riverboat and were joined there by one Alice Mitchel, a girl of 12 who was being sent to Grand Coteau to attend the Academy of the Sacred Heart, a girls' boarding school. The threesome made their way westward to New Iberia, traveling by train and by boat. From there, they boarded a stagecoach and began the journey to Grand Coteau. The roads were little more than dirt paths in many places. The ride was bumpy, and the dust came into the coach.

They reached Grand Coteau a day and a night after leaving New Iberia. Mary was impressed with the Academy of the Sacred Heart, a three-story brick building, with French-style gardens in front of it and with an alley of oaks leading to the Academy.

The morning after her arrival, Mary had just finished a breakfast of cornbread and molasses when Mother Victoria Martinez, the superior of the convent, pulled her aside for a talk.

"You must get strong and well quickly, so we can give you the veil," Mother Martinez said, referring to the white veil given to a postulant when she moves up to the stage of novice in the order.

"I'll do my best," said Mary, who, despite the distraction of poor health, remained optimistic and cheerful in the hope that she would soon wear the veil.

The veiling ceremony was set for October 20, 1866. But on the day before, Mary was stricken with an intense pain in the side and stomach. She hemorrhaged and began vomiting blood. She was hurried to the infirmary, and the doctor was summoned.

Dr. James Campbell rushed to the infirmary, and one of the nurses presented him with a sample of the blood vomited by the young woman. He examined it and concluded the girl had a disease of the stomach.

She hemorrhaged the next day and the next, and each time it happened she was drained of nearly all her strength.

On October 25, Dr. Campbell found her weaker than ever before. She had developed a disgust for food, even water.

Dr. Campbell, having been sick himself, and feeling unable to do justice to the patient, withdrew from the case. He was replaced on October 25 by Dr. Edward M. Millard, the regular convent doctor, who had been away.

Dr. Millard was considered to be a competent physician by the people of the community he had served for more than thirty years, but he was unable to do much to relieve the suffering of Mary Wilson. He stood by helplessly as her condition deteriorated.

Mother Martinez talked with Dr. Millard outside Mary's room the day after he took over the case. Having grown fond of Mary in the few months she had known her, Mother Martinez pleaded with the doctor to do something, anything, to ease her pain and suffering. But, Dr. Millard said regretfully, there was nothing he could do.

Mary's condition grew worse as the days passed. She was able to eat less and less food; the futility of administering medicine was confirmed time after time. Food and medicine only aggravated the girl's condition.

The nurses didn't try to give solid food again after November 7. On that day, Mary's attempt to swallow food triggered a violent fit of blood-vomiting and spasms that went on for twelve hours and that left the attending nurses weak in the knees. This attack, even more than the others before it, left Mary so weak and so still that one of the nurses thought the patient was dead. A priest was called in to administer the Last Sacrament.

The infirmarians, as well as many of the rest of the religious community, felt it was only a matter of time before the patient would expire.

Distressed at Mary's worsening condition, Mother Martinez decided to make a Novena to Blessed John Berchmans. The community would pray that God would cure or at least relieve Mary Wilson through the intercession of this Jesuit scholastic to whom two miracles had been attributed. He had died in Rome in 1621 at age 22 while studying to be a Jesuit priest. He needed one more miracle attributed to his intercession in order to be declared a saint by the Catholic Church.

For nine days the religious community would ask God to send John Berchmans to intercede on Mary Wilson's behalf to effect a cure or at least to relieve the sufferings of the dying girl. For nine days they prayed with this special intention in mind, the prayers always ending with the same words:

> Deign, O Lord, to glorify Thy servant, John Berchmans, by granting some relief to our suffering sister, and if her entire recovery be to the glory of the Sacred Heart of Jesus, grant it to our prayer, through the intercession of Blessed John, that thereby the cause of his canonization may be furthered.

A picture of Blessed John Berchmans was given to Mary, and one of the nuns came every day to recite the prayer at the foot of the bed.

The Novena started on December 6. The next day, Mary took a turn for the better, and the community rejoiced. But a day later, she took a turn for the worse. She rallied toward the evening, but the following day she plunged into the worst condition yet.

Feeling the end was at hand, Mary sent for Mother Martinez for some parting words. She said she was happy to be able to die in a house of the Society of the Sacred Heart, and she asked Mother Martinez to contact her parents and tell them that she had always loved them and would always love them.

Mary's eyes were closed now, and her hands and feet were cold and contracted. Her high fever continued; the vomiting of blood went on; the burning sensation in the intestinal area had spread to the throat and mouth; her tongue was swollen to the point that she could hardly be understood even when she had the strength to try to speak; the headaches persisted, and even chloroform failed to relieve them completely.

The doctor ordered the infirmarians to quit giving Mary any food, drink or medicine unless she specifically requested it. It would be inhumane to continue trying to force further administration of medicine or nourishment, he said. He had given up hope that she would be relieved, much less cured.

Mary bore the cross of her illness without complaining once. The doctor knew how much pain she was in by reading the involuntary expressions of bodily distress – the grimacing, the vomiting and the spasms.

"She's a brave girl," the doctor said to Mother Martinez. "She has suffered through all of this without a complaint."

"A martyr," Mother Martinez chimed in.

The last day of the Novena was December 14, and Mother Martinez hadn't slept much the night before. About dawn, she went to the infirmary, her eyes filled with tears. She opened the door to Mary's room then wept aloud at the pitiful sight. Mary's hands and feet were contracted, and she was drawn up in a fetal position, as if longing to be back in the protective shroud of her mother's womb. Her finger tips were blue, her tongue thick and raw, her lips discolored, her eyes closed, her mouth filled with dark, dried blood clotted around her teeth.

Mother Martinez entered the room and began weeping loudly and without restraint. She fell to her knees beside the girl's bed and begged God to allow her some relief.

"My child, would you like to receive Our Lord once more?" she asked.

Mary indicated she would. She tried to form a word, but her lips barely moved; she tried to nod her head, but it barely moved.

The priest came in and, seeing the condition of her mouth and tongue, placed only a tiny particle of the host on her tongue. He directed the nurse to give her a little water to help her swallow.

The effort to swallow brought on a pain so intense that Mary went into a convulsion, seizing the nurse by the arm and letting out a cry that chilled the people in the room. Then she lay back on the pillow, seemingly at peace.

All present left the room to attend Mass, knowing they could do nothing more for the dying girl.

After Mass, Mother Martinez returned to the infirmary. With tear-filled eyes, she peeked into the room before entering. She was flabbergasted.

Mary was sitting up in bed, the soreness in her mouth gone, her eyes open again and sparkling, her strength regained, very much alive and healthy, and smiling.

"Reverend Mother, I am well. I can get up," Mary said.

Mother Martinez was at once over-joyed and yet leery, thinking that perhaps she was seeing what was the last desperate burst of life that immediately precedes the death of some who have been suffering for a long period of time. But her fear was allayed when Mary began to tell her of the apparition of Blessed John Berchmans.

"After receiving communion this morning, being unable to speak, I said in my heart, 'Lord, Thou Who seest how I suffer, if it be for your honor and glory and the salvation of my soul, I ask through the intercession of Blessed Berchmans a little relief and health. Otherwise, give me patience to the end. I am resigned.' Then, placing the image of Blessed Berchmans on my mouth, I said, 'If it be true that you can work miracles, I wish you would do something for me. If not, I will not believe in you.'

"I heard a voice whisper, 'Open your mouth.' I did so as well as I could. I felt someone, as it were, put their finger on my tongue, and immediately I was relieved. I then heard a voice say in a distinct and loud tone, 'Sister, you will get the desired habit. Be faithful. Have confidence. Fear not.'

"I had not yet opened my eyes. I did not know who was by my bedside.... Then, standing by my bedside, I saw a figure. He held in his hands a cup, and there were some lights near him. At this beautiful sight, I was afraid. I closed my eyes and asked, 'Is it Blessed Berchmans?' He answered, 'Yes, I come by the order of God. Your sufferings are over. Fear not.'

"I opened my eyes, but he was gone. The sister infirmarian had gone down to the chapel to receive Holy Communion. I sat up in bed. I felt no pain. I was afraid it was an illusion and that my cure was not real. I turned over and over in my bed, without pain. I then exclaimed, 'It is true. Blessed Berchmans has cured me.'"

One of the infirmarians came in just as she finished telling Mother Martinez what had happened. She told the infirmarian, too, what had just occurred. To prove to her that she was no longer ill in the least, she asked her for a glass of water and drank it. The infirmarian believed her and was overwhelmed with emotion.

The word of the miracle spread through the community of Grand Coteau faster than any news ever had. It was received differently by different people, some believing it in its simplest form, others saying they'd believe it when they saw it, and others figuring that perhaps Mary's health had taken a dramatic turn for the better, but surely it had not been totally restored.

Dr. Millard arrived at about 8:30 that morning for his customary visit. He could hardly believe his eyes as Mary walked hurriedly to greet him, took him by the hand and sat him down for a talk.

"Is it really you?" he asked. He could believe that it was medically possible for her health to have improved to a great degree in a short period of time, but for him to understand how her disease could disappear without a trace, without any signs of convalescence, and to have gone from one extreme of health to the other in a period of forty hours, was beyond him.

"One thing is certain: If you are well, it is neither I nor my prescriptions that have cured you," he said after examining her.

At six that evening, Mary Wilson got out of bed and walked over to another bed so hers could be changed. The next morning she had chicken, toast, and coffee for breakfast. At 12:30 that afternoon she received permission to get up and get dressed. Then a stream of visitors began coming, thirty-five or forty of them. She prayed that afternoon in the chapel, and the whole religious community prayed with her.

On December 17, Mary Wilson received the habit of the Society of the Sacred

Heart in a ceremony that was attended by a sizeable crowd. Restored to health now, Mary began leading a normal life as a novice in her religious community at Grand Coteau.

About a month after the miracle, Mary was faced with the task of having to write her account of the miracle for presentation to the Archbishop of New Orleans. The archbishop, in turn, would study the material and forward it to the Vatican in Rome, where it would be examined. The canonization of Blessed John Berchmans hinged on the Vatican's acceptance of the miracle as authentic, and the acceptance of the incident as a miracle hinged in large part on what Mary

Sister Marie Greiwe (left) and Sister Odeide Mouton examine age-worn original documents attesting to the authenticity of the Miracle of Grand Coteau. The sisters were stationed at the Academy of the Sacred Heart at Grand Coteau when this photograph was taken in April of 1976. The rare documents were moved later to the Society of the Sacred Heart's National Archives in St. Louis, Missouri.

Wilson would write in her official attestation. She was writing her account of the miracle to the best of her ability but was concerned nevertheless that she might omit something that would make a difference in Rome.

On January 27, 1867, while Mary prepared her attestation, Blessed John Berchmans appeared to her a second time, to let her know he was satisfied with her statements, to urge her to be faithful to the rule of the religious order she had joined, and to inform her that she would die before her noviceship ended.

On August 14, 1867, Mary Wilson was stricken with a cerebral hemorrhage. She died three days later. She is buried in the convent cemetery at Grand Coteau. A shrine to Saint John Berchmans was erected in the room in the infirmary where the miracle occurred, on the second floor of the convent. Pilgrimages are made by thousands of people each year to the site of the Miracle of Grand Coteau.

The Shrine of St. John Berchmans is located on the second floor of the Academy of the Sacred Heart, in the same room where the Miracle of Grand Coteau occurred. Berchmans appeared to Mary Wilson in 1866 and was instrumental in her cure from a life-threatening illness.

*St. Charles College, originally an all-boys Catholic school, is today a retreat house and
novitiate for the 10-state New Orleans Province of Jesuits. Its intriguing history can be
divided into three distinct parts: It was a school for boys and young men from 1838 to 1922;
then exclusively a novitiate for the training of Jesuit priests and brothers from 1922 to 1972;
then both a novitiate and spirituality center, where retreats are made, from 1972 to the
present.*

Chapter Four

St. Charles College

SUNRISE AT GRAND COTEAU IS MOST BEAUTIFUL IN THE fall of the year when God paints the sky in brilliant hues of orange, pink and gold. It is this light that illuminates the huge white building known to many as St. Charles College and to others as the Jesuit Spirituality Center.

The imposing four-story brick structure looks like a building from another era. And, in fact, it is, having been constructed in 1909. It sits in the middle of a large, well-kept piece of property and, at this time of year at this hour of the morning, is surrounded by a light fog that lies upon the lawn like a soft, white blanket.

Morning is breaking, and people are starting to mill around. A group of five women are watching the sun rise over the old dairy barn that sits on the east side of the property. Two men in their forties are in rocking chairs on the front veranda, enjoying the crisp morning air and the quiet of the new day. Another man is walking up and down the long driveway that connects the college with the highway in front of it. On the east side of the college is a small parking lot filled with cars belonging to people attending a weekend retreat. Not far from the cars a woman in a heavy beige-colored sweater can be seen bending over picking pecans off the ground.

Inside the building are twenty-foot ceilings and wide hallways that run between rows of comfortably furnished dormitory rooms on three of the floors. Some people are headed down these halls to the showers. Others are just waking up, lying in bed and staring at the ceiling, thinking and praying. Others are gathered around the coffee urn in the cafeteria conversing softly about matters of the spirit.

Aerial view of St. Charles College provides a perspective on the size of the main building and the property upon which it sits. Behind the college and to the left is St. Charles Borromeo Church. The road in front of the college is La. Hwy. 93.

St. Charles College is a retreat house and novitiate operated by the Jesuits, members of a religious order formally known as the Society of Jesus. The college is a place where peace and quiet can be found, where rest and relaxation can be enjoyed. People come here from Louisiana and many other states to retreat from the hectic, material world. They come to think at an unhurried pace, to reflect on the direction of their lives, to satisfy their hunger for prayer and their search for answers. They seek nourishment for their souls and communion with the One who created them.

While the majority of retreatants are Catholic, like the Jesuits, many are people of other faiths, such as Baptists, Methodists and Episcopalians.

Two kinds of retreats are offered at the Spirituality Center. One is a retreat for groups of people and is held on the weekends, usually Thursday night through Sunday at noon. The other is an individual, one-on-one, silent directed retreat in which the retreatant consults daily with a retreat director who serves as an advisor and facilitator. This latter type of retreat is the primary mission of the center.

The group retreats, which attract from fifteen or twenty people to sixty or more, are led either by members of the staff of the Spirituality Center or by facilitators brought in from outside the center. In 2004, the staff included five Jesuit priests, two Marianite nuns, and one Vincentian priest.

The group retreat schedule includes Lenten retreats, Zen retreats and Anthony de Mello prayer workshops, as well as retreats with titles such as "Letting In The Love Of God," "Lessons Of The Heart," "A Vacation With The Beloved," and "Learning To Move In Harmony With Your Life." Some of these are silent retreats, and others are not. They include talks by the presenter, question-and-answer sessions, and group discussions. These retreats encourage participation and tend to bring about a special kind of bonding and spiritual camaraderie among the participants as they grow in understanding of the topic being discussed.

Directed retreats, on the other hand, are always silent retreats, with conversation between retreatants being considered out of line. Directed retreats are offered for three, five, eight and thirty days and are structured around the Spiritual Exercises of St. Ignatius Loyola, who founded the Jesuit order in the sixteenth century. (See related chapter, page 91.)

In defining a directed retreat, a flyer issued by the center points out:

> It is an opportunity for an individual to focus on one's personal relationship with God, particularly one's prayer life, as well as one's relationship with others. This is done over a period of time in solitude and silence in communication with God.

Weekend retreats at the Jesuit Spirituality Center cover an array of topics presented by staff members or facilitators brought in from around the country. **Above:** *Fr. James Dolan, S.J., travels from New York to facilitate Anthony de Mello prayer workshops.* **Below, left:** *Paula D'Arcy, a retreat leader and prolific writer of books, comes in from California to speak. Among her books are* Gift of the Red Bird: The Story of a Divine Encounter *and* Song for Sarah: A Young Mother's Journey Through Grief and Beyond. **Below, middle:** *Fr. Matt Linn, S.J., travels from Minnesota to give presentations rooted in Jesuit spirituality.* **Below, right:** *Sister Macrina Wiederkehr, O.S.B., comes in from Fort Smith, Arkansas, to lead retreats based on her Benedictine monastic spirituality and/or on her books. She has authored six books, including* A Tree Full of Angels: Seeing the Holy in the Ordinary *and* Gold in Your Memories: Sacred Moments, Glimpses of God.

Fr. Al Louapre, S.J., who was director of the center at the turn of the twenty-first century, points out that the teaching and experiencing of these Spiritual Exercises is the primary goal of the Jesuit Spirituality Center.

"The Spiritual Exercises help the retreatants to enhance their spiritual lives and to learn more about themselves and the nature of God," he observes. "We sponsor the weekend group retreats as a means of attracting more people to the center. We hope to draw many of these to make the one-on-one directed retreats, which are built around the Spiritual Exercises."

In all, five hundred to six hundred people make directed retreats here each year. The five-day retreat is the one made by more people than any other. The total annual attendance at the center comes to about 1,400 when the weekend retreatants are added.

Though it may not seem from casual observation that the center operates anywhere near capacity, the eight retreat directors are almost always busy, except from September through December. These directors usually consult with three or four retreatants per day. The busiest time is June, July and the first half of August, and additional directors are sometimes brought in during this period.

The center has rooms for fifty retreatants. When the demand is higher some people find lodging either at local bed-and-breakfast cottages or nearby motels. Others, who live in the area, simply sleep at home and drive in for the sessions.

Funding for the center comes from fees paid by retreatants, from two annual appeals sent to retreatants who have used the center, and from the Jesuits' New Orleans Provincial Office.

*   *   *   *   *

In addition to being a center for retreats and spiritual direction for lay people, St. Charles College functions as a novitiate for the training of future Jesuit priests and brothers.

Here, in the novitiate, they are introduced to the life of the Jesuit, spending two years in a program of prayer, study and apostolic works to help them decide whether they want to commit to this way of life.

The novitiate is not merely a school for academic learning, but a place for spiritual training and discernment. St. Ignatius, founder of the Jesuit order, envisioned the novitiate as "a school of the heart," a place where men would develop their interior life, their prayer life. From the novitiate, the men in training would be

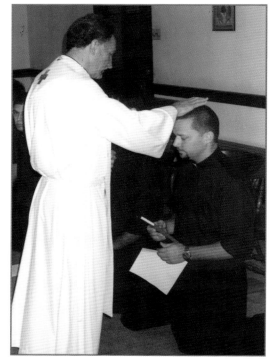

Jesuit novice John Brown receives a blessing from Fr. Warren Broussard, S.J., director of the Jesuit Spirituality Center. Both the Jesuit novitiate and the spirituality center are housed in St. Charles College.

sent out to do apostolic works, such as teaching, working to improve the lives of the poor and homeless, and proclaiming the Gospel of Jesus Christ through their words and their deeds. In doing so, they would come to know, with some degree of certainty, whether the life of the Jesuit is for them.

In this same spirit, the novices at St. Charles College today spend about half of their two-year novitiate period away from the college doing apostolic work. Some spend a few months in Tijuana, Mexico, working with sisters to feed the poor; others go to U.S.-Mexico border towns to visit the imprisoned and work on behalf of the homeless; others spend time in a remote village of El Salvador working with a Jesuit priest and ministering to the needs of the natives in various ways, both material and spiritual. Each novice experiences three or four placements, or missions, during his two years in the novitiate.

They are also sent to high schools for a couple of months to do substitute teaching, counseling and tutoring.

In addition to the apostolic work, the novices study the Constitutions of the Society of Jesus and, at the end of their two-year novitiate, make their vows of poverty, chastity and obedience.

The novitiate is only the beginning of the long, ten- or eleven-year process of becoming a Jesuit priest. The next phase is three years of study of philosophy and some theology; then a stage called regency, which is a two- or three-year period of work, often teaching high school; then three years of study of theology; and finally ordination to the priesthood.

St. Charles College has been the novitiate for the New Orleans Province of Jesuits since 1922. The novitiate had been located in Macon, Georgia, since the 1880s, but that facility was destroyed by fire in 1921; then St. Charles College was

Jesuit novices in the novitiate at Grand Coteau are involved not only in academic pursuits but also apostolic works. **Left:** *Novices John Brown (left) and Jeff Johnson visit a home-bound resident of the Grand Coteau area.* **Above:** *Novices Luis Blanco (left) and Jeremy Zipple visit an elderly woman in McAllen, Texas, while on an apostolic mission.*

designated the province's novitiate. The province is comprised of ten Southern and Southwestern states.

Down through the years, hundreds upon hundreds of men have come through the novitiate at St. Charles College. While the number in the program was much higher in its heyday, in the 1940s and '50s, the Jesuits still maintain a vital novitiate, with an average of twelve men in the program at any given time.

The three lives of St. Charles College

Since its opening in 1838, St. Charles College has come through a long and interesting sweep of history. The Jesuits who resided here in the nineteenth century witnessed several epidemics of yellow fever, the coming and going of slavery, the occupation of Grand Coteau by both Union and Confederate troops during the Civil War, and the celebration of the Miracle of Grand Coteau, which occurred through the intercession of a fellow Jesuit. Later generations of Jesuits were here for the destruction of the college by fire, for the buildup and decline of a massive farming operation that fed those living in the college, and for the tide of refugees who poured into the town during the Great Flood of 1927.

The colorful history of the college can be divided into three distinct parts, or eras. First, it was a school for boys and young men for eighty-four years, from 1838 to 1922; second, it was exclusively a seminary for the training of Jesuit priests and brothers for fifty years, from 1922 to 1972; third, it was and is both a seminary and spirituality center where directed retreats and weekend retreats are made, beginning in 1972 and continuing today.

A school for boys and young men (1838-1922)

The Jesuits first came to Grand Coteau in 1837 at the behest of the Bishop of New Orleans, Rev. Antoine Blanc. A severe shortage of priests in the remote parts of his diocese prompted the bishop to travel to Rome in April of 1836 to meet with the Superior General of the Jesuits and to request that he send several Jesuits to the untamed reaches of Louisiana.

Accordingly, six priests and two brothers – all of them French-speaking – were sent from the Province of Lyon, France, arriving at the port of New Orleans in February of 1837. They were welcomed by Jesuit superior Fr. Nicholas Point.

Fr. Point was at this time in the process of deciding on a location to establish the first Jesuit college in the South. While he was considering several communities, he selected Grand Coteau because of the shortage of priests in the area, as well as the complete lack of Catholic education for boys. One thing that tipped the scale in favor of Grand Coteau was the offer of a huge piece of property by Mrs. Charles Smith, the same woman who had donated the land on which the Religious of the Sacred Heart had established the Academy of the Sacred Heart in the previous decade. Another major factor that attracted the Jesuits was that the Religious of the Sacred Heart had in 1821 established a school for girls in this remote location, proving it was a viable place for Catholic education.

The nuns wholeheartedly approved of the Jesuits settling in as their neighbors because no other priests were stationed here permanently, which meant they were able to receive the Sacraments and attend Mass only intermittently. That situation would change if the Jesuit fathers made Grand Coteau their home. Not only did the sisters approve of the Jesuits coming to Grand Coteau, but they prayed for it – and campaigned for it. As early as 1832 the superior of the convent was writing letters to her Bishop requesting that "the sons of Loyola" be sent to Grand Coteau.

While Fr. Point was trying to decide where to locate the college, the superior of the convent, Mother Bazire, stepped up and offered a special incentive for the

The original St. Charles College building was constructed in 1837-38. It was destroyed by fire in 1907.

Jesuits to settle in Grand Coteau: 200,000 bricks, free of charge. The bricks had been made in the nuns' brickyard for a chapel they intended to build, but they were willing to donate the bricks to help build the college if the Jesuits would choose Grand Coteau.

That did it! A mountain of free building materials, a huge plot of free land, a real need for their services as priests and teachers, and a community that would welcome them with open arms: This was too sweet of an offer for any reasonable person to turn down. Fr. Point said "yes," and the Jesuits headed for Grand Coteau.

In July of 1837 construction was begun on the school and a residence for the priests and brothers. The newly arrived Jesuits planted a mile-and-a-half-long alley of oak trees from the site of the college to the Academy of the Sacred Heart, signaling their intention to work in unison with the nuns for many years to come.

The college was named for St. Charles Borromeo (1538-1584), a Bishop of Milan and noted church reformer. The Jesuits are said to have selected this name in part because the property donor's late husband, Charles Smith, was named for this saint and had a strong devotion to him.

St. Charles College opened in January of 1838 with fifty-six students and grew to more than one hundred in a few years. The "college," which provided academic and religious training of boys and young men, included three divisions: a primary school, a secondary school, and a junior college.

Students came from Lafayette, New Iberia, Opelousas and other south Louisiana communities that were relatively nearby, as well as from New Orleans and points east. Entries in the St. Charles College Minister's Diary attest to the fact that the Jesuits went to great lengths to recruit students to assure the success of the school. An entry dated January 20, 1840, notes, "Fr. Abbadie arrives from New Orleans with seventeen boys;" another, dated October 10, 1841, says, "Fr. Abbadie arrives with sixteen boys from St. Michael's." Jesuit priests or brothers would meet the boys at an appointed time and place and accompany them on the long, sometimes arduous journey to the college, via riverboat, flat boat and stagecoach, and in later years by train.

The curriculum in the early days was made up of reading, writing and arithmetic, humanities, rhetoric, philosophy and religion.

In the early going, and intermittently through its history, the college was plagued by any number of problems, not the least of which were shortages of money and manpower to teach. Only six years into their noble experiment the rector of the school was on the verge of despair from a chronic, seemingly insurmountable financial malaise. The Minister's Diary – a journal of significant events occurring at the college – records that he called a meeting on July 18, 1843, to inform the townspeople of the "sad condition of finances and deplorable state of our college." To remain open, he said, the college would need seventy to eighty students. In response to his appeal, the concerned citizens agreed to write letters to encourage their friends to send their children to the college.

Going through several financial ups and downs, the college reached a record high 128 students in 1856. In response to this growth, a second building was constructed near the first in 1858.

Like other people living in rural America, the Jesuits contributed to their own support and that of their students by growing their own food, including corn, beans, sweet potatoes and various fruits. Dairy cattle supplied milk, beef cattle supplied meat, and herds of sheep provided wool to be sold for cash. The Jesuits struggled through their first quarter of a century in Grand Coteau, part of the time with the help of a few slaves, who cooked, did household chores and worked in the fields. This arrangement ended abruptly, however, for the Jesuits and for other Southerners, with the onset of the Civil War in 1861.

The imminence of war began the process of destabilization of the economy, deflation of the value of the currency, and reduction of the student population of St. Charles College. The promise of war sent the anxiety levels of the populace soaring. New Orleans fell to the Union army in April of 1862, then the Yankees moved westward into the Teche Country.

On April 19, 1863, Union Gen. Nathaniel Banks established a camp near Chrétien Point, near what is now Sunset, a few miles west of the college. He soon sent a cavalry detachment to the college, summoning its president and presenting him with a certificate of "special protection of the United States." This protection applied to "the college and convent, their inmates and property," as well as to the town of Grand Coteau in general and all its citizens.

Meanwhile, Gen. Banks' men, an army of some 30,000, were camped out in the fields and meadows around Grand Coteau and nearby Sunset. From this base of operation, they moved north to capture Opelousas easily, fighting off half-hearted Confederate resistance.

Approximately six months later, on November 1, 1863, another Union battalion marched through the town, causing quite a disturbance. The sound of drums and the blare of bugles startled the Jesuits, their students and townspeople who were attending Mass.

Under the command of Gen. William Franklin, the troops camped in the fields near Grand Coteau and prepared to engage the enemy. Two days later Union and Confederate forces faced off in the Battle of Grand Coteau, also known as the Battle of Bayou Bourbeaux. There was significant bloodshed on both sides. Union war documents reported 25 Union soldiers killed, 129 wounded, and 562 taken prisoner. Some of the Jesuits witnessed part of the battle from the fourth-story windows of the college, and just down the road the nuns were watching the fighting from their second-story balcony.

St. Charles College managed to make it through the war without having to close, but it was in bad shape financially as its student population had dwindled to about fifty. One Jesuit who taught at the college throughout the war, Fr. C.M. Widman, observed later:

> The college came out of the war with a heavy debt, which the subsequent years could only increase, as the expenses were very great, the numbers of scholars growing smaller every year.... We all had suffered much – less indeed than most of the poor people, soldiers, women, and children – but withal had great reason to praise God for the singular protection we experienced.

The grueling war finally ended on April 9, 1865, with the surrender of Gen. Robert E. Lee at Appomattox, Virginia. A few days later, President Abraham Lincoln was assassinated. Skirmishes continued in Louisiana for another two or three months.

While much of the post-war news in the Grand Coteau area could be described only as discouraging, if not depressing, one local event did occur in December of 1866 that lifted the spirits of the people and built the faith of many. It was the famous Miracle of Grand Coteau, in which Mary Wilson, a young postulant in the Society of the Sacred Heart, was cured of a life-threatening illness through the intercession of Blessed John Berchmans. Berchmans was a Jesuit scholastic who had lived in Diest, Belgium, and had died some two and a half centuries earlier. His role in the miracle led to his canonization.

The following year was not a happy one for hardly anyone in south Louisiana. As if the depressed post-war economy was not enough to burden the populace, the area was visited by an epidemic of yellow fever, as it had been several times before and during the war. In August of 1867 the fever was raging in nearby New Iberia, and one of the priests traveled there to minister to the dying. In October yellow fever took the lives of two Jesuit priests who were stationed at the college, Fr. Francis Nachon and Fr. Anthony deChaignon. Neither of the funerals was well attended due to the prevailing panic over the dreaded fever; people stayed home and prayed that they and their loved ones would be spared.

Bad news continued in 1868. In the latter part of the year, after many years of financial hardship and other adversity, the Superior of the Jesuit Province ordered the college closed, much to the dismay of the staff and students.

Good news followed only a few months later, however, as townspeople learned that the previous decision had been reversed and that the school would be re-opened. The reason: The Jesuit school in Mobile, Alabama, Spring Hill College, had burned to the ground, and the priests, brothers and students needed a school. So, they moved to St. Charles College, and school was again in session. This arrangement lasted for about a year, then Spring Hill re-opened and the visiting students and faculty returned to Alabama.

St. Charles College continued to operate as before, though part of the facility was converted to a novitiate for Jesuits-in-training in 1872. The novitiate functioned in Grand Coteau for fifteen years, until 1887, when a new novitiate for the

Members of the faculty of St. Charles College pose for a picture next to one of the college buildings in 1894. Black cassocks and birettas were standard attire for Jesuit priests at the time.

The present St. Charles College, as it appeared in 1910, was completed in 1909 after fire destroyed the original buildings, one in 1900 and the other in 1907.

New Orleans Mission was opened in Macon, Georgia.

Another yellow fever epidemic hit Grand Coteau and much of the South in 1897, but the inhabitants of St. Charles College survived it and headed for the new century with a feeling of optimism.

Unfortunately, however, the big news of 1900 was fire on the campus; the building that was constructed in 1858 was destroyed in a spectacular fire that threatened nearby buildings as well. The good news was that the eighteen Jesuits who lived in the building escaped with their lives. With only one classroom building remaining, the college was able to function only as a day school for students living in the immediate area. This is the way it was until 1907, when another fire took down the remaining building, the original one, built in 1837.

Determined to not be defeated, the Jesuits dug in and built a larger, more modern facility at Grand Coteau, graciously rejecting offers from the governmental leaders of New Iberia and Lafayette to build the school in their towns. The college was rebuilt in 1909 and blessed by Archbishop of New Orleans James Blenk in a ceremony that is reported to have been witnessed by a crowd of 2,000.

For thirteen years after its dedication, the new college building continued to function as a school for lay students. Eventually it housed more than a hundred boarders, who were joined by fifteen to thirty day students. To the students and their parents, the future of the college seemed bright, the operation stable and prosperous.

But life is filled with illusion, and with circumstances beyond the control of any but a few. It was in May of 1922, at the end of the school year, that St. Charles College ceased being a school for lay students. It was to become exclusively a novitiate and juniorate for the training of men studying to become Jesuit priests or brothers. One reason given for the discontinuation of classes for lay students was that the Jesuit novitiate in Macon, Georgia, was destroyed by fire the previous year and the Superior of the New Orleans Province decided to move the novitiate to Grand Coteau. Another reason was that the number of colleges and universities in the South – including Loyola University, founded by the Jesuits in New Orleans in 1912 – was growing, and these institutions were sure to draw students away from St. Charles College, thus bringing about another round of financial debilitation and stress. The handwriting was on the wall, so to speak.

Despite tough times for much of its existence as a school for lay students, St. Charles College was ultimately quite successful in its mission to provide a quality education, both secular and religious, for boys and young men. This is why the Jesuits came to Grand Coteau eighty-four years earlier, and this is what they did, albeit sometimes by the hardest. They turned out generation after generation of young Christian men who were well-equipped in mind and spirit to make positive, meaningful contributions to the world into which they graduated.

A novitiate for the training of Jesuit priests and brothers (1922-1972)

For much of its storied history St. Charles College has had an aura of mystery about it, but never more so than during the fifty-year period when it was exclusively a novitiate, from 1922 to 1972.

During this time there were no lay students attending classes. Townspeople and other visitors didn't feel free to come onto the property at will. Occasional retreats brought small numbers of lay people and religious onto the grounds and into this house of mystery. Motorists from nearby communities drove past the college and wondered what went on inside those walls.

The college was like an island in the midst of the community of Grand Coteau. It seemed to exist in a world of its own.

What most of the public knew for sure was that this was a place where men came to study to be Jesuit priests and brothers. Many must have wondered what that entailed, but few had much information about the process or the curriculum. What did the novices do with their time? What did they study? From where did they come? Where did they go when they left the novitiate?

For forty-five years of this fifty-year period (1922-1967), St. Charles College functioned as both a novitiate and a juniorate, serving as the young Jesuits' home for the first four years of their training. Since 1967 it has been a two-year novitiate. A novitiate is a place where novices (prospective priests or brothers) spend their first two years studying, discerning and generally being introduced to the way of life of the Jesuit order. At the end of this period they take their perpetual vows of poverty, chastity and obedience. A juniorate is a place where "juniors" spend their next two years in serious academic training. In the past they focused on Latin, Greek, composition and history; nowadays the emphasis is on English, modern foreign languages and humanistic studies.

At its peak, from the late 1940s through the 1950s, there were 120 people living in the college. There were approximately fifty men in the novitiate and forty in the juniorate, plus a number of priests who taught and administered and ten or twelve Jesuit brothers. The brothers were in charge of things such as the laundry room, the kitchen, the infirmary, the treasurer's office and the farming operation. In addition, there were several elderly and retired priests living in the house.

With this many people living here, the house was busy from well before dawn until well after dark. Classes in spirituality, English, Greek, Latin and other subjects were being taught by the priests and attended by the novices and juniors. Mass was being celebrated daily, and practically everyone in the house was in attendance. The brothers were busy washing, rinsing and hanging the clothes on the clotheslines outdoors. With so many people to feed three times a day, the kitchen workers – who were among the few non-Jesuits in the house – were busy preparing food much of the day. The farming of sweet potatoes, sugarcane, beans, corn and other crops was being done by a few Jesuit brothers and townspeople but with much assistance from the novices. The dairy, built in 1925, was being managed and worked by Jesuit brothers; Holstein cows were supplying the house with lots of fresh milk, and the excess was being sold for cash.

For the most part, the Jesuits remained in the house or on the grounds; the novices and juniors seldom left the property, and never without permission. It was something of a monastic existence, like the lifestyle of the Benedictines, who remained in the monastery and helped to support the household by working at various tasks. However, the Jesuits' quasi-monastic way of life would change in the 1960s following the Second Vatican Council, when the various religious orders around the world were directed to return to their roots, to go back to the style of spirituality of their founders. The style of St. Ignatius, founder of the Jesuits, was apostolic (going out and teaching and helping), not monastic (staying home and praying and working).

The farming operation was no small enterprise, with some 800 acres under cultivation during one season or another. Broad and deep expanses of land were planted to sweet potatoes; their vines and leaves covered the long rows for as far as the eye could see looking northward from the college toward the Academy of the Sacred Heart. Jesuit novices were given the job of planting sweet potato vines and digging up mature sweet potatoes at harvest time. It was tough manual labor that

Members of the Jesuit juniorate faculty at St. Charles College get together for a picture in 1937. Left to right are Fr. Tom Carter, S.J.; Fr. Francis Xavier Entz, S.J.; Mr. Leonard Larguier, S.J.; and Mr. Gus Coyle, S.J.

For many years the Jesuits operated a major farming enterprise on their property to feed the men who lived in the college. Jesuit brothers and a few townspeople headed the operation, with help from novices, raising corn, beans, sweet potatoes, sugarcane and other crops. **Above:** *The dairy barn, built in 1925, is where the cows were milked, beginning in the wee hours of the morning.* **Below:** *Modern equipment was used to reduce the drudgery of farm work where possible.*

built not only muscle, but also humility and character.

In the autumn, at harvest time, a group of twenty to thirty novices could be seen heading for the fields to dig sweet potatoes following an early breakfast. A tractor would go into the fields the day before and turn up the rows to loosen the dirt so the potatoes could be extracted more easily. Each novice would take a row, kneel down next to it, and start digging with his bare hands.

For two, three, maybe four hours, they would dig and dig and dig, until they reached the end of their row. As they worked their way down their row, they'd leave the potatoes between the rows, and one of the overseers would come behind them and separate the potatoes by size, weight and shape and place them into different crates accordingly. The crates would be carried to the headrow, placed in a pickup truck, then hauled away for the potatoes to be washed.

Tired and dirty, the novices would trudge out of the fields and back to the big house to bathe, change clothes and rest before going to the noon meal, and later to class.

The novices also harvested sorghum, which was used for feed for the livestock, and great quantities of pecans, which were sold commercially for a time. Strawberries, figs, corn and various citrus fruits were also grown for the residents of the college.

Digging up sweet potatoes was perhaps the toughest farm work for the aspiring Jesuits. It was not what one would call a labor of love, by any means, but an exercise in the vow of obedience. Fieldwork wasn't an elective subject, and it is doubtful that many of the strapping young novices would have opted for it if they had their druthers.

Nevertheless, they must have taken some pleasure in the abundance of the harvest. They supplied the kitchen with enough sweet potatoes to feed the entire house at practically every meal for several months each year. The bulk of the potatoes were sold for cash, to help support the college.

*   *   *   *   *

If the college was somewhat isolated from contact with the general public for much of its tenure as a novitiate, that condition would change abruptly with the coming of the Great Flood of 1927.

Because the college and much of the community of Grand Coteau are situated on a ridge – which is very high ground compared with most of the land in this region of Louisiana – hundreds of refugees fleeing the floodwaters poured onto the Jesuits' property, bringing their cars, trucks, wagons, buggies, mules, horses and cattle with them.

Though the Jesuits were aware of the flooding upriver, in the northern part of Louisiana, and they fully expected to be visited by some refugees, they were not prepared to receive so many people with so many animals. But, of course, they responded with charity and compassion, feeding the hungry, clothing the half-naked, and extending a hand of friendship and comfort to their weary, frightened neighbors, most of whom they had never met.

In December of 1926 and January of 1927, news of flooding began to trickle in as heavy rainfall in mid-America caused the Ohio River to overflow, which in turn pushed the Mississippi River to unusually high levels. Heavy rains in Louisiana in February and March further pushed the capacity of the Mississippi River. In April the levees paralleling the Mississippi River started to break in Arkansas and Mississippi; in May the same happened in north Louisiana, then in south Louisiana. A big percentage of the Mississippi River's flood waters headed down the Atchafalaya River, quickly overflowing its banks, breaking its levees, and sending thousands of farmers and residents of small communities scrambling for higher ground.

A Jesuit novice studies in the quiet and solitude of his room, circa 1940-50.

In all, some 72,000 people who resided on the western side of the Atchafalaya River took to the roads leading west; 21,000 refugees ended up in Lafayette and 14,000 stayed in refugee camps in Opelousas. Some 2,400 refugees came through Grand Coteau and camped in nearby Sunset, and a few hundred stopped in Grand Coteau, many of whom camped on the grounds of St. Charles College.

St. Charles College was designated a Red Cross Center, to help with what would surely become a massive relief effort. Fr. Michael Grace, the rector of the college, was appointed chairman of the three committees – food, health

Fr. Michael Grace, S.J., minister of the novitiate at St. Charles College at the time of the Great Flood of 1927, played a major leadership role in providing relief for refugees from the flood. The tranquility and isolation of the semi-monastic Jesuits residing in the college at the time was changed abruptly as hundreds of people and their livestock poured onto the college grounds.

and livestock – for his area.

Fr. Grace opened the Jesuits' pastures to 1,100 cattle, but heavy rains, coupled with the ramblings of the cattle, turned the pastures into mud. Next, he donated much of the hay that the Jesuits had been storing for their own cattle. When this hay was gone, about a week after the arrival of the refugees, the visiting cattle were driven northwestward to grazing lands around Ville Platte.

Some of the refugees lingered in Grand Coteau well into July, waiting for the waters to recede and for the Red Cross to give the word that it was safe to return to their homes, or what was left of their homes and farms.

For the Jesuits, things weren't back to normal at the college until all their visitors were gone, more than two months after they had arrived. For the refugee farmers, things would not be back to normal for many months, if ever. Some returned to their farms only to find their barns washed away by the flood and their houses collapsed or tilting badly.

*   *   *   *   *

The following year, 1928, was highlighted by the building of a grotto honoring Our Lady of Lourdes, just behind the college. And just beyond the grotto a new Jesuit cemetery was laid out. The original Jesuit cemetery, which is located a little way to the northeast, within the community cemetery, was full, with graves dating back as far as the 1840s.

The centennial of the Jesuits' presence in Grand Coteau came around in 1937, and with it came a major announcement by Bishop Jules Jeanmard, Bishop of Lafayette. He revealed plans for the Diocese of Lafayette to build a facility that would be used exclusively for retreats to be directed by Jesuit priests. The building would be erected just north of the new Jesuit cemetery – on the site of the original parish church – and it would be called Our Lady of the Oaks Retreat House. When construction was completed the new facility would be turned over to the Jesuits to be operated by them. And so it was, in 1938.

Fr. Sam Hill Ray, S.J., was the first director of Our Lady of the Oaks. He actively recruited Catholic men to make retreats at the new facility, creating a system of team captains in each area of the diocese. The captains, in turn, recruited others to attend, and a retreat movement was begun, filling the new twenty-five-room facility each time. Down through the years the retreat house would be enlarged two or three times, bringing the capacity to fifty rooms, and offering retreats for

A grotto honoring Our Lady of Lourdes was built in 1928 between the college and St. Charles Borromeo Church. It remains a favorite place of prayer for some Jesuits, retreatants and townspeople.

Novices, juniors, priests and brothers gather for a meal in the Jesuit novitiate's dining room at St. Charles College, circa 1950. At its peak, in the 1940s and '50s, some 120 men lived at the college; the number began to decline in the 1960s.

men, women, married couples and clergy.

The 1940s, '50s and '60s constituted a golden era for the Jesuits at Grand Coteau. While lay people filled the new retreat center to capacity, young men were entering the Jesuit novitiate in strong numbers, at an unprecedented rate. By 1960, the number of novices and juniors had grown to about one hundred, filling the college to its limit. To make room for more aspiring Jesuits, the college was expanded. A new wing was built, including a larger dining room and kitchen on the ground floor and a large chapel just above it.

Shortly after the new wing was built, however, came a reversal in the trend of growing numbers of men entering the priesthood. This was the case not only at St. Charles College but for seminaries throughout the United States. Consequently, in 1967 the juniorate program was discontinued at St. Charles College and moved to Spring Hill College in Mobile, Alabama. The two-year novitiate program remained and continues today.

The Jesuit Spirituality Center
and Novitiate (1972 to the present)

In the late 1960s and early '70s, at about the same time that the number of men entering the seminaries was going into a significant decline, a new retreat movement was gaining momentum around the world.

It was a movement revolving around the giving and making of directed retreats based on the Spiritual Exercises of St. Ignatius. This movement was given life partly as a result of the deliberations of the Second Vatican Council. Leaders of the Council had directed the superiors of the various religious orders – Jesuits, Franciscans, Dominicans, etc. – to go back and examine and imitate more closely the spirituality of their founders.

In the case of the Jesuits, a major part of the spiritual practices of St. Ignatius Loyola was the giving of one-on-one directed retreats in the form of the Spiritual Exercises. Over the centuries the Jesuits had gotten away from this style of retreat, opting instead for what seemed to be the more time-efficient preached retreat, wherein a priest could preach to thirty or forty or more retreatants at one time.

With the latter form of retreat already being practiced at Our Lady of the Oaks Retreat House, leaders of the Jesuits' New Orleans Province decided to make St. Charles College into a Spirituality Center, open to the public. Its primary purpose would be the promulgation of the Spiritual Exercises of St. Ignatius, to be given and received on a one-on-one basis.

And so in 1972 the college was designated the Jesuit Spirituality Center. It would also continue as a two-year novitiate for the training of future Jesuit priests and brothers.

Conclusion

While St. Charles College is a place with three relatively distinct lives, it has been entirely consistent through more than a century and a half in promoting the teachings of Jesus Christ as the way, the truth and the life.

Originally drawn here as promulgators of the Catholic faith, the Jesuits have succeeded in their various missions: to provide Catholic education for lay students, to train men in their early years of formation as Jesuits, and to give the Spiritual Exercises to men and women seeking a richer relationship with God.

After all these years, the college remains a holy place and a place of mystery. This

At a special Vow Mass in St. Charles Borromeo Church in August of 2004, nine Jesuit novices made their vows as they continued on the journey toward the priesthood. **Facing page:** The Mass was concelebrated by more than 30 priests, led by Jesuit Provincial Fr. Alfred Kammer. **Above:** Following the Mass the novices gathered for a picture with Jesuit priests. Left to right are Fr. Francis W. Huete, Novice Director; Luis Blanco; Fr. Paul Deutsch, Provincial Assistant for Formation; Casey Metcalf; Patrick Hough; Quang Tran; Eric Ramirez; Raul Navarro; Jeremy Zipple; Dominic Nguyen; Fr. Alfred Kammer, Provincial Superior; Peter Zagone; and Fr. Michael Dooley, Assistant Novice Director.

venerable building is a nearly indelible symbol of the Jesuits' presence in south Louisiana and their commitment to the teachings of the Gospels. The age of the building, the beauty of its surroundings, the knowledge of what has gone on inside its walls for decades: These things tend to inspire confidence and trust in this place called St. Charles College and in the religious order that has operated it for all these years.

It is with this same confidence that people from all walks of life continue to make retreats here. They come in search of a more meaningful spiritual life. They come to pray, to rest their minds and bodies, and to nourish their souls.

St. Ignatius Loyola (1491-1556), founder of the Society of Jesus, dedicated all that he did "to the greater glory of God" (Ad majorem Dei gloriam) and spent much of his life leading others to the Spiritual Exercises. These same Exercises are the foundation of the retreats offered at both retreat houses in Grand Coteau today.

Chapter Five

St. Ignatius and the Spiritual Exercises

THE PRIMARY MISSION OF THE TWO JESUIT RETREAT centers in Grand Coteau is the giving and making of the Spiritual Exercises of St. Ignatius, a form of contemplative prayer designed to bring a person into closer communion with God.

The preached retreats at Our Lady of the Oaks and the guided retreats at St. Charles College both are based on the Spiritual Exercises, which were written in the sixteenth century by St. Ignatius Loyola.

The founder of the Jesuit order, Ignatius spent much of his life helping others to pray with faith and perseverance, using the Spiritual Exercises.

The giving of Spiritual Exercises retreats by Jesuits continues today not only at Grand Coteau but all over the world. The Exercises can fairly be thought of as Ignatius' gift to the world, or, perhaps more accurately, a gift from God, received by Ignatius and passed on to people of faith in his generation and every generation since.

Now, St. Ignatius was no saint at all when he was a young man. Born into Spanish nobility, the last of thirteen children, he was quite fond of drinking, gambling, dueling, soldiering and the chasing of women. He is said to have been enthusiastic toward all of these pursuits. He was a man of the world, a soldier who craved recognition for his valor, and he relished his role in life.

His pursuit of honor and glory was cut short, however, when he was severely injured during a military encounter with the French. He and a few hundred Spaniards were defending Pamplona when shrapnel from a cannonball struck him in the legs, causing serious injury. He was returned to his family's castle at Loyola, where he began a long period of recuperation. To pass the time, he wanted to read books about chivalry and romance, but none could be found in the castle. What was available were books on the life of Christ and of the saints, including St. Francis of Assisi and St. Dominic. So, he read these books and pondered their mysteries.

As he read and reflected on the content of the books he began to see the folly of the ways of the world. He began changing his mind about what mattered most in life. He was experiencing a change of heart as he considered the heroic virtue of the likes of Francis and Dominic.

It was the first time Ignatius had read the stories of these two saints, and he was moved by their profound love of God. He admired their prayerful, disciplined lives, their charity toward their neighbor, their respect for the Church's authority, and their untiring work to create religious orders whose purpose ultimately was to praise God and to teach others to live in accordance with the Two Great Commandments.

Ignatius saw that Francis and Dominic were soldiers, too, but for a cause more worthy than the killing of one's neighbor in the name of an earthly king. How much more noble would it be to help another toward eternal salvation rather than to take his life on the field of battle? Ignatius began to wonder whether he too could make a meaningful contribution to the building of the Kingdom of God, and the thought of it filled him with joy. The idea of working for the greater glory of God, rather than for his own glory, brought him a deep and lasting sense of consolation.

Ignatius read the life of Christ carefully and slowly, and at some point it started to sink in that Christ had died for him, personally, so that he could enjoy eternal life. If that were not enough to bring about a complete change of mind and heart, Ignatius had a vision of the Blessed Virgin Mary with the child Jesus, images epitomizing the virtues of purity, innocence and holiness.

During this period of conversion he developed a great revulsion for sin, particularly sins of the flesh, which had been one of his specialties. He became disgusted at the thought of the unholy, materialistic, self-serving life he had led. It was now time to do penance, and he resolved to make a penitential journey to the shrine of Our Lady of Montserrat, which was not far away.

He arrived at the Benedictine monastery at Montserrat in March of 1522 after exchanging his fancy, expensive clothing for beggar's garb, such as was commonly worn by those doing penance. He purchased a piece of brown sack cloth, which a tailor fashioned into an ankle-length garment; he also acquired sandals, a pilgrim's staff and a canteen for water. He gave up his sword and dagger for good, leaving them before the Shrine of the Black Madonna. He remained at the monastery for a few days, confessed his sins to a priest, and spent most of the night on his knees in prayer.

From Montserrat he went to nearby Manresa, where he took up residence at a hospice for the poor, doing what he could to help others less fortunate than himself. By day, he attended Mass at the local Dominican priory and begged on the streets for his daily bread. Some weeks after his arrival, he was invited to stay in the monastery, in a small room, an offer which he accepted. Soon after moving into the monastery he discovered a cozy little cave in the hills on the outskirts of town. It became his second home; he spent countless hours and even days at a time, withdrawn, secluded, praying. Near the cave was a swift-flowing stream called the River Cardoner. He would spend hours by the water, observing nature and starting to see God's creative hand in everything around him.

On some days Ignatius, the hermit, could be seen limping into town to beg for food. His hair, beard and fingernails had grown to a length that seemed unreasonable to some of the townspeople. His clothing was dirty and needed to be washed in the worst sort of way. But Ignatius was in the process of becoming a true contemplative, with matters of profound importance on his mind, and he certainly was not concerned with anything so frivolous as what people might think of him or his appearance.

Though he was indifferent to the stares of his well-groomed neighbors, Ignatius was still heavily burdened by a guilty conscience. He was living through "the dark night of the soul." He prayed with great resolve, but nothing seemed to be happening in his heart, mind or soul. It seemed that God wasn't listening.

Deeply remorseful over the life he had led, Ignatius fell into depression and despair, going so far as to think about suicide. But he persisted in prayer, begging the Lord for his help and his mercy.

Ignatius carried with him a little notebook, frequently making notes of his attempts to reach God through prayer and contemplation. He meditated on the nativity and on the crucifixion and on the resurrection, keeping Jesus always on his mind. He continued to immerse himself in prayers of gratitude for graces received and to ponder the events of Christ's passion. He prayed and wrote and prayed and wrote and prayed some more.

So deep and earnest was his prayer that at some point, somehow, he experienced the very presence of God. It was in September of 1522 on the bank of the River Cardoner outside his cave. The experience was utterly indescribable, unimaginable, unlike anything Ignatius ever thought possible. In that special moment of grace, that brief direct encounter with God, Ignatius received divine inspiration, a privileged insight into and understanding of supernatural mysteries that cannot be fathomed by mortal man through any natural means.

It was as though he was now imbued with a new intellect, a mind different than the one he possessed when he arrived at Manresa. In this visionary experience he came to a new understanding of the creation of the world; from now on he would find God in all things.

On another occasion, while praying on the steps of the monastery in Manresa, he was divinely inspired in his understanding of the Holy Trinity. Once during Mass in the monastery Ignatius had a vision of Christ as the priest elevated the host during the consecration, leading him to a clear understanding of the dual nature of Christ, both human and divine.

These mystical experiences unleashed an even greater fervor for prayer and a boundless energy for writing about what he was experiencing when he prayed. So, he continued making notes and writing, and writing, and writing. And thus was born the Spiritual Exercises of St. Ignatius, the product of persistent prayer and divine inspiration.

After more than a year living in Manresa, Ignatius made a pilgrimage to the Holy Land, longing to see and touch the sacred ground upon which Jesus had walked. From there he returned to his native Spain, to Barcelona, where he spent a couple of years in the classroom to bolster his very limited education, including the study of basic Latin. In his early thirties at the time, Ignatius was in class with boys twenty years or more his junior. He was keenly aware of the inadequacy of his schooling, and he knew that a solid education would make him better equipped to go forth into the world and contribute to the building of the Kingdom of God. He may have felt a bit awkward and somewhat humbled to be in the classroom with children, but this was a price he was willing to pay to reach his goal.

From Barcelona, he moved on to the universities in Alcala and Salamanca, but he spent practically as much time in jail as he did in class. His enthusiasm for preaching and interpreting the Gospels and for sharing the Spiritual Exercises with others got him in trouble with the Spanish Inquisition. Inasmuch as Ignatius was not an ordained priest at the time, he was charged, in essence, with preaching and teaching without a license. Representatives of the Inquisition were always nervous about the theological utterings of free-lancers, regardless of what they were saying. Concerned with even the possibility of the spreading of heresies, they tended to lock up anyone whose authority to preach was in question. Not one to be locked away quietly, the divinely inspired prisoner continued to preach from behind bars, and groups of people stood outside the jail to hear what he had to say.

Ignatius moved on to the University of Paris in 1528 and settled down for seven years to study theology, philosophy, literature and Latin grammar. It was here, in Paris, that he attracted and won over his first six companions, including Peter Faber, Francis Xavier, Alfonso Salmeron, Diego Lainez, Nicholas Bobadilla, and Simon Rodrigues. These men played a major role in the establishment of the Jesuit order.

Most of the companions, including Ignatius, were ordained in 1537. Ignatius said his first Mass about a year later, on Christmas Day of 1538, in Rome in the Church of St. Mary Major in the Chapel of the Manger.

The order was formally approved by Pope Paul III and begun in 1540; Ignatius was elected as its first Superior General the following year. It was a job to which he was completely devoted, laboring from sunup to sundown, and then some. He oversaw the drafting and perfecting of the Constitutions of the Society of Jesus, directed Jesuit priests to every corner of the earth, and stayed connected with them by the writing of thousands upon thousands of letters. The early Jesuits established schools, built churches, founded parishes and did every manner of mission work on every continent. Their teachings and preachings were rooted in the Spiritual Exercises, just as they are today. All of their work, ultimately, had a single purpose and was dedicated *ad majorem Dei gloriam*, "to the greater glory of God," just as it is today.

Ignatius was never happier and more fulfilled than when he was giving the Exercises, or "helping souls," as he liked to say. Though his days were more than filled with the responsibilities of overseeing a rapidly growing religious order, Ignatius made the time to continue giving the Exercises until shortly before his death in 1556.

*   *   *   *   *

The Spiritual Exercises are a collection of spiritual activities including prayer, meditation, scriptural readings, examination of conscience, and acts of self-denial,

Ignatius of Loyola had several mystical experiences as his prayer life deepened and as he moved toward the founding of the Society of Jesus. **Facing page:** *At Manresa, Spain, on the bank of the River Cardoner, Ignatius experienced the very presence of God and gained insights into supernatural mysteries.* **Right:** *In Rome, while he was establishing the Jesuit order, he had a vision of Christ and God the Father.*

all designed to strengthen one's spiritual health, thus drawing the person closer to God. Just as physical exercise will strengthen the muscles of the body, so too will spiritual exercise strengthen the person's spiritual life and health.

The Spiritual Exercises originally were designed by Ignatius to be given by a director, usually a priest, to one other person over a period of thirty days. This one-on-one style is used today at St. Charles College and other spirituality centers around the world; it is referred to as a directed retreat. These retreats may go for three, five, eight or thirty days. (Another form of directed retreat is referred to as the Nineteenth Annotation retreat, wherein the retreatant makes the Exercises not at a retreat house but at home or elsewhere, meeting with a director weekly to discuss the spiritual movements and growth he/she is experiencing.)

A second style of Ignatian retreat, referred to as a preached retreat, is given to a group of as many as fifty or even more persons by a priest or other retreat director. This is the type of retreat that is given at Our Lady of the Oaks, as well as other retreat houses around the world. These usually last for three days. Several talks, grounded in the Spiritual Exercises, are given by the retreat director; afterward the retreatants spend time reflecting on the essence of the talks, usually with the aid of related scriptural readings.

In any case, the substance of the Spiritual Exercises retreat today is essentially the same as Ignatius outlined it in the sixteenth century. It begins with The First Principle and Foundation:

> The goal of our life is to live with God forever. God gave us life because he loves us. Our own response of love allows God's life to flow into us without limit.
>
> All the things in this world are gifts of God, presented to us so that we can know him more easily and make a return of love to him more readily.
>
> As a result, we appreciate and use all these gifts of God insofar as they help us develop as loving persons. But if any of these gifts becomes the center of our lives, they displace God and so hinder our growth toward our goal.
>
> In everyday life, then, we must hold ourselves in balance before all of these created gifts insofar as we have a choice and are not bound by some obligation. We should not fix our desires on health or sickness, wealth or poverty, success or failure, a long life or a short one. For everything has the potential of calling forth in us a deeper response to our life in God.
>
> Our only desire and our one choice should be this: I want and I choose what better leads to God's deepening his life in me.

In all, there are more than two hundred specific exercises grouped into four sections, or "weeks," so-named because the Exercises were originally given and made over a four-week period. The sections can be summarized as follows:

Week One: A prayerful study of who God is and how special the individual human being is in God's eyes, the goal being to come to know God more intimately and to appreciate him more fully. This phase includes reflection on how people throughout history, ourselves included, have failed to respond to God's love in a positive way, i.e., the committing of sin. The object here is not only to understand but to feel God's love for us — in spite of the fact that we are sinners.

Week Two: Prayer and meditation on the life of Jesus, from his infancy through his public life, the goal being to enter into a deeper relationship with him as we come to know him better, love him more, and grow in our desire to serve him and to follow him more closely.

Week Three: Contemplation and prayer on Jesus' suffering, crucifixion and death, for our sake.

Week Four: Prayer and reflection on Jesus' resurrection from the dead and his appearance to people afterward as he returns to console and encourage his followers. This final exercise is intended to bring us to a state of gratitude for all that Jesus and God the Father have done for us.

So, here it is, half a millennium after Ignatius wrote the Spiritual Exercises, and this form of prayer is still being shared with people on every continent on the face of the earth. The Exercises continue to have the power to change the hearts and strengthen the spirits of men and women who approach them with a modicum of faith and perseverance. They are shared in Paris, Manresa, Barcelona and Rome; they are made in Dallas, San Francisco, New Orleans and Grand Coteau.

Ignatius' fondest wish was that others could experience the presence of God as he did for much of his life following his conversion. Ignatius must be smiling. He is getting his wish as people of generation after generation have continued to search for and to find the Holy One through the Spiritual Exercises.

Our Lady of the Oaks Retreat House is a place where men and women retreat from the hectic, material world to relax, to take stock of their lives, and to commune with God in silence. The driveway leading to the facility is lined with oak trees and the Stations of the Cross.

Chapter Six

OUR LADY OF THE OAKS RETREAT HOUSE

JESUIT PRIESTS FIRST ARRIVED IN GRAND COTEAU IN 1837 TO minister to the fledgling Catholic population of the area. They tended to the spiritual needs of students and teachers at the nearby Academy of the Sacred Heart and founded St. Charles College as the first Jesuit-operated college in the South.

Though the Jesuits began directing retreats for the religious and laity of the region at St. Charles College in 1872, it was not until 1938 – exactly 101 years after they first arrived – that a facility was designed and built exclusively for retreats. It is called Our Lady of the Oaks Retreat House, and it is still going strong today, attracting some 3,000 retreatants per year, primarily from the thirteen-parish area of south Louisiana that comprises the Catholic Dioceses of Lafayette and Lake Charles.

Our Lady of the Oaks is a facility that invites people to walk away from the world for a three-day weekend – to retreat from the hustle and bustle of everyday life – to come to a peaceful, restful place that will help them relax and pray and get in touch with themselves and with God.

Built in a Spanish Mission architectural style, the facility encloses a courtyard with a fountain in the middle that is shaded by century-old live oak trees. An oak arcade lines the driveway leading to the front of the building. Behind the retreat house, in an oak grove overlooking a wide pasture, is an old Jesuit cemetery containing headstones dating as far back as the mid-1800s. On one side of the retreat house is another cemetery, for the community of Grand Coteau in general. On the other side is another, newer Jesuit

The interior courtyard of Our Lady of the Oaks Retreat House is a peaceful spot, with a fountain and benches in the center and oak trees on either side. There's no unwelcome noise here, only the relaxing sounds of birds chirping, squirrels chattering and water falling in the fountain.

cemetery, the historic St. Charles Borromeo Church, St. Ignatius School, and a wide, shaded walkway leading to St. Charles College.

The retreats at Our Lady of the Oaks are silent retreats; retreatants are required to be silent and to listen to what God may have to say, rather than talking with one another. The booklet handed out at the start of the retreat addresses the subject:

> All important is total silence during the retreat. There is no way to make a good retreat unless you are recollected, and no way to be recollected without silence. It is the best way "to listen to God and respond." It is itself a great prayer: "Be still and know that I am God." (Psalm 46)

The silence of the retreat replaces the noise and stress of everyday life. There are no radios or TV sets, no cell phones, no nagging kids or complaining co-workers, no fighting to get through congested traffic, nor hectic schedules, nor tight deadlines.

The sounds one does hear are the chirping of birds, the chattering of squirrels, and the laughter of children at play on the adjacent school ground. Retreatants do pray aloud when they are attending Mass, saying the Rosary, or praying the Way of the Cross. They also talk to the priests privately during confessions and one-on-one consultations. A few times per day they hear the retreat director giving brief talks and instructing them to read the Bible passages that relate to these talks. Otherwise, the only other sound is that of an old-fashioned bell ringing to wake them at 7 a.m., or pealing at noon as retreatants pray the Angelus.

Our Lady of the Oaks was built by the Diocese of Lafayette under the direction of then-Bishop Jules Jeanmard. It was turned over to the Jesuits as a gift, in appreciation for a century of service to the diocese and its people.

When the facility was dedicated, in October of 1938, the bishop expressed hope that "the laity will make the retreat house a beehive of spiritual activity." The record shows that his hope was and is being realized.

Bishop Jeanmard noted that funding for the facility came primarily from money left to the diocese in the wills of Msgr. Amable Doutre and Fr. A. J. Maltrait, plus a sizeable donation from Msgr. A. F. Garneau. The building was constructed at a cost of $40,000; it accommodated twenty-five retreatants. A second story was built in 1951, increasing the capacity to forty-two retreatants. Today the facility accommodates fifty.

The first director of Our Lady of the Oaks was Fr. Sam Hill Ray, S.J. He zealously promoted retreats, traveling the length and breadth of the diocese, talking to Knights of Columbus and other laymen's groups, using his natural charm and personal magnetism to win over "converts" to what he and others referred to as "the retreat movement."

One strategy Fr. Ray used to build and maintain the number of retreatants each year was the creation of a network of retreat captains throughout the diocese. These are people who promote the retreats by reminding those in their charge to sign up for the retreats and recruiting new people to join the movement. The captain also serves as a liaison between the retreat director and the retreatants while the retreat is underway.

Considerable credit for the early success of the retreat movement is also due to the Knights of Columbus councils of the diocese. In the 1940s they inaugurated a program encouraging and supporting retreats. This was the beginning of the Laymen's Retreat League, which has continued to promote retreats through the years.

For many years retreats for high school juniors and seniors were included in the schedule; however, these were discontinued in the 1970s when a different approach was developed for this age group.

The schedule of retreats now includes retreats for men, for women, for married couples, and for clergy.

The retreats given and made at Our Lady of the Oaks are based on the Spiritual Exercises of St. Ignatius, founder of the Jesuit order. (See related chapter, page 91.) These retreats are properly referred to as conference, or group, retreats because they

Statues on the grounds

The grounds of Our Lady of the Oaks Retreat House are accented with statues of some of the saints. **Left to right:** *St. Ignatius Loyola, founder of the Jesuit order; St. John Berchmans, who was instrumental in the Miracle of Grand Coteau; St. Joseph with the Child Jesus; and St. Francis Xavier, one of St. Ignatius' original companions.*

involve a retreat director addressing a group of fifteen, twenty or even fifty people. By comparison, the style of retreat given and made at the nearby Jesuit Spirituality Center at St. Charles College is called a one-on-one directed retreat and involves a director working with one to five single retreatants, one at a time. These retreats, too, are based on the Spiritual Exercises. The Spirituality Center also hosts various weekend retreats for groups.

'Weekend Miracles'

The power of the Spiritual Exercises retreats to change people's minds and hearts for the better is demonstrated week in and week out at Our Lady of the Oaks. Jesuit priests who have given these retreats for many years regularly observe this phenomenon.

For instance, Fr. Frank Coco, S.J., who has been involved in retreat work for more than three decades, speaks enthusiastically about what he refers to as "weekend miracles." The following three stories are among his most memorable recollections:

• A young woman attending a retreat around 1995 had missed a few of Fr. Coco's talks in the chapel. He noticed her, looking dejected and depressed, sitting in a rocking chair outside of her room, so he went up to her and asked if she was okay.

"I'm just so distracted, so restless. I can't keep my mind on this retreat. I lost my baby recently, and I just can't seem...," she said as tears slid down her cheeks.

Fr. Coco could see she needed to talk, so he invited her to his office. Her despair, depression and profound sense of loss were apparent as she told the story of the death of her baby, crying pitifully all the while.

Just being able to talk about it helped her a lot, and after that visit with the priest she attended the remaining talks. When the retreat was over she seemed to be at peace. There was even a sense of joy about her – exactly the opposite of her demeanor at the beginning of the retreat.

• A businessman (call him John) arrived on a Thursday evening to begin his retreat. He was dismayed to see his former business partner (call him Harry), whom he considered a bitter enemy. And the feeling was mutual. They avoided even eye contact with one another and welcomed the silence of the retreat.

In one of his talks, the retreat director spoke about Jesus' message of forgiving your enemies and doing good to those who hate you. John was moved by what he heard, and he decided to try to reconcile with Harry. So, despite the rule of silence, he knocked lightly on Harry's door, went in, talked with him, and offered an apology for his part in the acrimony. They forgave one another, shook hands, and left the retreat that Sunday afternoon as men with changed hearts.

• A friend of Fr. Coco's named Ronnie Dupont called him with panic in his voice one day in 1985.

"I need to talk to you. Can I come right now?" he said.

A jazz pianist who lived in New Orleans, Ronnie drove to Grand Coteau immediately. The man was burdened with despair, depression and marital problems. He was drinking heavily, and he had not been to church in a number of years. He was despondent over the death of his 10-year-old son, who had died the year before from "huffing," i.e., the practice of inhaling gases from aerosol containers with the intention of getting high.

Fr. Coco and Ronnie had known each other since the mid-1960s, when Fr. Coco, a clarinetist, would occasionally sit in and play with the Pete Fountain band, of which Ronnie was a member.

Ronnie arrived on a Thursday morning and proceeded to tell Fr. Coco of his miserable life, his out-of-control drinking, his disastrous marriage, and his acute feelings of loneliness and loss. Fr. Coco consoled and sympathized with the man, and when Ronnie was finished telling his sad story, Fr. Coco invited him to stay for a retreat, which was starting that afternoon. Though he had no intention of

Fr. Kenneth Buddendorff, S.J., director of Our Lady of the Oaks Retreat House, celebrates Mass in the chapel. Fr. Buddendorff is the founder of a program in which lay men and women are trained to be retreat directors.

participating in a retreat when he arrived, he felt called to do so.

"Why not? What have I got to lose?" he said sadly.

So, he stayed and attended the retreat. He enjoyed the food, and the silence, and the beautiful environment. He found peace and serenity for the first time in a long time. And he cried when he prayed.

Fr. Coco was the director of that retreat, and much of what he said during his talks really registered with Ronnie.

"Every time Fr. Coco spoke to the group I felt he was speaking directly to me, about me. He really connected," Ronnie said.

The talks, the prayers, the rest, the time to reflect, all of these things combined for a memorable and life-altering experience.

"That experience changed my life. If I hadn't gone there, I swear, I'd be dead now," he said, referring to his previous inability to stop drinking. "Fr. Coco saved my life."

Ronnie arrived at Grand Coteau half-drunk; he left sober, with no desire to drink whatsoever, and he abstained from alcohol completely for the better part of twenty years.

"I feel like I truly came in contact with God when I was at Our Lady of the Oaks. I understood for the first time in my life that I wasn't really alone, that God was with me. And he still is," Ronnie reported. "I'm really not afraid of death anymore, nor am I afraid of being alone."

Commenting on these memorable episodes at Our Lady of the Oaks, Fr. Coco offers the following observations:

"These are three of the many weekend miracles of grace that I have witnessed as, at age eighty-three, I continue in my thirty-fourth consecutive year in the conference retreat ministry. Of the many people who attend retreats here, surely some come just for the ride, never scratching below the surface of their lives. Some come with heartaches and find healing of the spirit. Some come in need of liberation and find freedom of heart. Some, at peace with God, neighbor and themselves, come simply to reflect, pray and learn to walk more closely with the Lord.

"The most consoling aspect of this fruitful ministry – in which so much can happen in so short a time – is those weekend miracles."

Lay men and women sharing retreat director duties

The directing of retreats at Our Lady of the Oaks had been the exclusive domain of Jesuit priests since the retreat house opened in 1938. But that changed in 2002 with the introduction of lay retreat directors.

Now, some of the retreats are given by lay men and women who have completed a two-year course called the Internship in Spiritual Direction Program. The program – which is in keeping with the spirit of the Second Vatican Council that calls the laity into fuller participation in the life of the Church – is designed to help sustain the retreat movement at Our Lady of the Oaks and elsewhere. The program at Grand Coteau was founded by Fr. Kenneth Buddendorff, S.J., retreat director at Our Lady of the Oaks. He launched a similar program at Montserrat Retreat House in Dallas in 1999. The program is modeled after one that has been offered in New Orleans since the 1980s.

The training of lay men and women as retreat directors was made necessary by the declining number of men entering the Jesuit priesthood nationwide since the 1960s. If this trend continues, there will be fewer and fewer priests available to direct retreats in the future, so the laity are being called upon to help staff this ministry.

Retreating from the hectic, material world

Whether it is clergy or laity giving the retreats, the number of men and women attending the retreats is strong. Most sessions are either full or nearly full. A large

Fr. John Condry, S.J., a veteran retreat director at Our Lady of the Oaks, says the retreat movement across the country is growing in part because more and more people are realizing the ultimate futility of spending most of their lives in pursuit of material wealth.

percentage of the retreatants return year after year; it is not uncommon to learn of men or women who have attended retreats here for ten, twenty or even thirty years.

Fr. John Condry, S.J., one of the Jesuits who staffs Our Lady of the Oaks and who has been involved in retreat work for more than two decades, says people return to the retreat house regularly because their experience is spiritually and psychologically satisfying.

"The retreat movement is growing here and at other Jesuit retreat houses across the country because people are tired of the purely materialistic world," Fr. Condry points out. "Chasing and acquiring material things doesn't meet their spiritual needs. It leaves them unfulfilled, empty inside. So, they come here in search of spiritual enrichment – and they find what they are looking for."

The retreat experience at Our Lady of the Oaks can be thought of fairly as one continuous prayer, a spiritual exercise designed to draw a person into a more meaningful relationship with God.

"The whole idea of attending retreats is to engender a closeness to God, a friendship that keeps maturing and becoming richer. And I think people are able to find that here, so they return year after year," Fr. Condry concludes.

*A crucifix overlooks the old Jesuit graveyard behind Our Lady of the Oaks Retreat House.
This spot, just outside the gate to the cemetery, is a favorite place for retreatants to pray,
especially in the early morning when the cross is seen in silhouette against the beautiful colors
of dawn.*

Chapter Seven

Coming Home to a Quiet and Simple Place

I
T IS STILL DAYLIGHT, THOUGH LATE IN THE AFTERNOON, WHEN
the men from Lafayette begin arriving for their annual retreat at Our Lady
of the Oaks. The cars come in slowly, making their way from the narrow highway
to the retreat house by way of a long driveway lined with the Stations of the Cross
and covered by a canopy of venerable oaks. It is Thursday, October 31, 2002, and
the autumn sun bathes the place in a golden light.

The men park their cars in front of the retreat house, then carry their over-
night bags and hanging clothes to their rooms. They go into the library to sign in
and are greeted by the retreat captain and fellow retreatants. Conversations
develop about their children, or their duck hunting trip, or about the war that
seems to be coming between the United States and Iraq, or about the New
Orleans Saints' chances of making it into the playoffs. Mostly, though, the talk is
about the retreat.

"Boy, I need this one in the worst sort of way," says one man in his sixties,
dressed in a light blue shirt and maroon tie.

"It's so good to be here again. I can't believe it's been a year...," says another
fellow in his forties, leaning back in his chair at the registration table.

Men in their forties and fifties continue to trickle in, and before long a dozen
guys are in the small library, talking, laughing, bonding. There's lots of hand-
shaking and some hugging. By now the sun has set on Grand Coteau, and the
headlights of another car can be seen in the driveway heading toward the retreat
house.

111

Many of these fellows, the younger men and the older ones, seem tired and burdened when they arrive for the retreat. Some look forward to being able to go to confession or to hear the priest's talks about eternal salvation, while others speak with enthusiasm about being served three square meals a day or being free to take a nap whenever they want. They all come, consciously or unconsciously, in response to Jesus' standing invitation: "Come to me all you who are burdened, and I will give you rest."

After the men have signed in, it's time for supper, which always starts at seven on the first night of the retreat and which always consists of red beans and rice and sausage, plus salad and French bread. If the supper is familiar, so are the faces of the women who prepare and serve the meals. Always dressed in white kitchen attire, most of these women have been here for twenty to thirty years. They smile when asked how long they've been on the job; they answer with pride in their voices.

It is permissible for the men to talk during this first supper, but not for the duration of the three-day retreat, except at the last meal, on Sunday at noon. Silence is an indispensable part of the retreat. It is required if a person is to tune out the things of the world, to allow the stresses and distractions of everyday life to fade from the conscious mind — and thus to allow true communication between the retreatant and God.

The literature placed in every retreatant's room contains a sheet that addresses the importance of silence. It states:

> Silence creates the climate of interior stillness in which God's voice can be heard. Abstaining from dialogue with others unleashes the easy, spontaneous communication with God which is prayer.
> Silence enables us to make contact with our innermost self and thus satisfy our anxious quest for self-identity, inner freedom and self-determination. It also enables us to explore the purpose of life, probe more deftly our fundamental options, and tap the deep resources of human power which each one has but seldom uses....
> Silence is therapeutic. It eases tension and helps us to relax. It offers a welcome, soothing relief from the nerve-racking noise pollution of the city.... Silence enables us to communicate intelligently.... Without periods of silence we can only babble.

After supper, and after a brief orientation meeting in the chapel, the men retire to their rooms in silence to unpack, to settle in, to read or pray for a while before going to sleep. The rooms are simple and uncluttered, with a bed, a rocking chair, a small desk, a pen and tablet for journaling, a Bible, and a crucifix on the wall. The very simplicity of the room is conducive to relaxation. It's a cordial little space that embraces and welcomes its occupant. No phone, no TV, no daily newspapers with stories of strife, controversy and conflict. None of that matters here in the peaceful confines of this room. It is good to begin to withdraw from the world, good to be coming home to a quiet and simple place where relaxation and communion with God are the order of the day.

At seven o'clock in the morning the old-fashioned bell on the edge of the courtyard rings and wakes up anyone who still might be sleeping. Most retreatants are awake already, walking around the grounds, having coffee in the dining room, or sitting in a rocking chair on the porch outside their room. One or two men can be found behind the retreat house at dawn, praying before the crucifix that overlooks the old Jesuit cemetery. The graves here contain the mortal remains of members of the Society of Jesus, the Jesuits, who have served the spiritual needs of the people of south Louisiana as far back into history as the 1830s. The headstones are engraved in Latin.

At 7:40 the men gather for morning prayers in the chapel, then file quietly into the adjacent dining room for breakfast. Near the entrance is a little wooden sign engraved with the words "Silence is Golden." All of the men are observing the letter and the spirit of the rule of silence.

Following the blessing of the meal the retreatants are seated, and the head dining room attendant turns on some background music. She plays "How Great Thou Art" and "Make Me A Channel Of Your Peace," followed by a beautiful rendition of "Hail, Mary," which sounds as though it is being sung by angels.

The food is brought to the tables by the servers, and it is passed around from one retreatant to the next, without any talking. This morning the menu features cereal, grits and scrambled eggs, but, being Friday, no meat. If one man wants the milk which is out of his reach he only points to it and another man passes it to him.

The dining room is clean, well-lighted and even cheery, with high ceilings and exposed beams that are painted a light cream color. Following the meal, the usually active and talkative men sit quietly, listening to the music and staring into space or looking out the sliding glass doors toward the community cemetery. For the most part, they seem quite content, this group of about forty-five men who come from all walks of life.

Among them are a clean-shaven doctor in his late forties with a half smile and an amused look in his eye; a retired university professor who spent some years in the seminary studying to be a priest; ten or twelve guys in their twenties and thirties, some of them attending their first silent retreat; an aging black man with an abundance of snow white whiskers who keeps rubbing his chin; a rugged Hell's Angels type guy with his head shaved and with an angelic look on his face; a tired-looking businessman in his fifties who keeps staring at the food remaining on his plate; and a rather large fellow in his sixties with a protruding belly, folded arms, a shaved head, a slight pout and looking like Buddha with wire-rimmed glasses.

After breakfast the men fan out. Some head for their rooms, others go for a walk, a few take a seat on the benches around the fountain in the courtyard.

The weather is perfect, about sixty degrees, clear skies and low humidity. The fountain is surrounded by pots of purple and gold chrysanthemums. The men on the benches listen to the water as it trickles from the top pool of the fountain to the lower pool. They're resting their minds, just listening to the water fall. They can see a squirrel on the grass at the foot of one of the oak trees inside the courtyard; it chatters from time to time as it nibbles on the corn left out by the groundskeeper. Midway up the tree are two blue jays pecking around for insects on a branch, but the men don't seem to notice.

During a silent retreat the pace of life slows down, giving way to the tempo of nature. There's no hurrying here. You can feel the tension of life melting away as the body and mind relax and the weighty matters of the world fade into oblivion. You are able to become present to yourself, and then to God.

The lecturer for this retreat is Fr. Joe McGill, S.J.

The mortal remains of many of the Jesuit priests and brothers who served in the Southern United States are buried in two cemeteries in Grand Coteau.
Facing page: *A replica of the crucified Christ overlooks the old Jesuit graveyard behind Our Lady of the Oaks Retreat House. A second, more recent Jesuit cemetery is located nearby, behind St. Charles Borromeo Church.* **Right:** *Headstones in the old Jesuit cemetery are engraved in Latin.*

Fr. Joe McGill, S.J., one of the retreat directors at Our Lady of the Oaks, relaxes in his office between presentations. In the tradition of Jesuits around the world, he is a learned man with a formidable command of theology, philosophy and the art of teaching.

He's 72 years old and has been a Jesuit most of his life. He's an Irishman with crystal blue eyes, a ruddy complexion and just a little white hair remaining on his head. He enters the chapel wearing black pants and a black long-sleeved shirt with the white Roman collar of a priest. He genuflects reverently in the direction of the tabernacle, though his old knee does not make it all the way to the floor.

"What keeps us from experiencing the love of God in the fullest sense is the noise within us that drowns out his voice," Fr. McGill begins, explaining that this noise is the tension between the natural and supernatural programming in all of us.

God's nature is to give of himself, and since we are made in the image and likeness of God, we receive this "divine imprint," this supernatural genetic coding, to do likewise – to be loving and self-giving, Fr. McGill explains.

Human beings are also born with an instinct for self-preservation, so we all receive this "natural imprint." We are thus programmed for self-preservation, he says.

"The tension between the natural and supernatural can be hard to handle. So we try to anesthetize ourselves to the tension. We sometimes try to erase it through excesses of sex, booze, pills, even work or exercise – whatever we attempt to lose ourselves in to relieve the tension," he submits.

So, how should a person deal with this tension?

"Acknowledge it, recognize it is there, make peace with it, and make a habit of being loving and self-giving toward your neighbor," Fr. McGill suggests.

A by-product of the instinct for self-preservation is anxiety over the thought that when we die we will cease to exist. This fear, of course, springs from the "natural imprint" and is completely at odds with the "divine imprint," which teaches that the soul is immortal, that it will live forever.

"This clash of opposite ideas creates the noise that prohibits us from recognizing more fully that it is in self-giving, not self-preservation, that we find our reality and our hope," Fr. McGill concludes.

He leaves the retreatants with a final thought: Anxiety is the exclusive domain of human beings; notice that the birds of the air are not anxious about what tomorrow may bring.

Then he gives the men a reading assignment of several Bible passages related to his talk. One is from the Gospel of St. Matthew (6:26-34), quoting Jesus:

> Look at the birds flying around; they do not plant seeds, gather a harvest, and put it in barns. Your Father in heaven takes care of them! Aren't you worth much more than birds? Which one of you can live a few more years by worrying about it?
>
> And why worry about clothes? Look how the wild flowers grow: They do not work or make clothes for themselves. But I tell you that not even Solomon, as rich as he was, had clothes as beautiful as one of these flowers....
>
> So do not start worrying: "Where will my food come from, or my drink, or my clothes?" ...Your Father in heaven knows that you need all these things. Instead, be concerned above everything else with his Kingdom and with what he requires, and he will provide you with all these other things.

The retreatants file quietly out of the chapel, going off in several directions. Two or three head for the benches around the fountain in the courtyard. They lean back on the benches, communing with nature, hearing the fountain's water falling, and listening to the chirping of the carefree birds.

Half an hour goes by, and the retreatants on the benches are greeted by a small dog, which moseys into the courtyard – another of God's creatures who doesn't seem to know anything about work or worry. It seems that the dog had a little time on his hands, so he dropped by just to see who was lounging around the fountain today. The black and brown dog looks like a miniature schnauzer with a natural hairdo, which is to say, he could stand a trip to the dog groomer.

One man tries to shoo-away the shaggy dog, apparently feeling that dogs don't belong at retreats.

Another man invites the dog to come closer, stooping down and extending a welcoming hand, apparently feeling there is a place at retreats for animals. If birds and squirrels can come, why not dogs?

Like birds, dogs have something to teach us. Could it be that they're little angels, sent by God to serve as living examples of unconditional love? Once a dog starts to love and depend on you, he'll be faithful till the end. When you come home from work or school, his heart seems to leap for joy the moment he sees you. He barks, spins, twirls, and tries to jump in your arms. Even if you're tired or in a bad mood or disinterested, he's still glad to see you. If you are not bearing gifts or treats, it doesn't matter, he's still wagging his tail. His enthusiasm over seeing you again is boundless; his love, unconditional.

In addition to what a dog can do for a person's sense of self-worth, having a dog and spending time with it can make us into better human beings. A person who learns to be kind to animals cannot be unkind to his fellow human beings. Patterns of kindness, compassion and patience that we acquire through our dealings with our pets can be extended to our dealings with other people.

So, there is a place for dogs at retreats, inasmuch as they have something to teach us. Why, they could even be considered part of the staff.

The old bell at the edge of the courtyard tolls again, beckoning the men to the chapel for another session of theology with Fr. McGill. Joe McGill, who is one of the four priests stationed at Our Lady of the Oaks, is a Jesuit through and through, a man learned in theology, philosophy and the art of teaching. In the tradition of Jesuits around the world, he is sharp and conversant, possessing knowledge and insight way beyond that of the average Joe. He's the kind of guy you'd want on your team if you were debating anyone, at any time, on any topic of theology or philosophy. Intellectual attributes aside, he is gentle and compassionate as he proceeds through his presentations. He is in his element now, doing what he was put on this earth to do, as he steps to the podium to talk about how to deepen one's relationship with God.

"Jesus said, 'Blessed are the poor in spirit, for theirs is the Kingdom of Heaven,'" Fr. McGill begins, explaining that the term "poor in spirit" entails acknowledging and experiencing our powerlessness, emptiness, helplessness.

He is quick to point out that to be poor in spirit, to embrace this virtue, runs completely counter to our natural human tendency to secure our positions in life and to continuously try to build our material wealth. Here again, the tension continues between the natural and the supernatural, the taking nature versus the giving nature.

"In the quest for eternal salvation, the 'minimalist position' is merely to try to keep the Ten Commandments – doing just enough to get by," he explains.

The "maximalist position" is quite different.

"This is true Christianity, evidence of the divine imprint, giving of ourselves to God and our neighbor without condition," he says. "With this, we are not attached to any person, place or thing. We are devoted to God and motivated only by self-giving and by love of God and neighbor."

The retreatants are sitting quietly and attentively as Fr. McGill completes his lesson. The message is sinking in. Fr. McGill picks up his notes from the podium and walks out of the chapel. Most of the men remain. This minimalist versus maximalist comparison gives them something to think about.

It's 11:30 a.m., half an hour before lunchtime. The skies are clear and it's a dry sixty-five degrees. The men have settled into the mode of silence and are feeling at home now, and all is well at Our Lady of the Oaks Retreat House. From the gazebo, just outside the chapel's side door, you can see the cattle in the far field, grazing at their usual speed, which is no speed at all. The pace of nature prevails.

Just beyond the near fence is Grand Coteau's community cemetery. Here and there you can see people placing flowers on the graves. A woman in a straw hat is bent over and painting a grave. Today is All Saints Day, November 1, and tomorrow is All Souls Day, and it is customary throughout south Louisiana to sweep and wash and even re-paint the graves of loved ones. This activity is not only a gesture of love and respect for the dead, but also a testament to the people's faith, their belief that their departed loved ones are alive, that their souls live on in heaven.

One of the retreatants, a fellow who looks to be 40 or 45, strolls by the gazebo, then walks along the near fence. He looks like he's deep in thought, his hands in his blue jean pockets and looking down at the ground. He seems to be at peace, as do many of the men who are milling around the grounds.

Three men are sitting on the benches around the fountain in the courtyard, listening to the water fall and noticing the birds as they hop between the branches of the great oak trees. The birds don't seem to have a care in the world. Neither do the men.

Four saints or saints-to-be are known to have visited the Academy of the Sacred Heart at Grand Coteau. Rose Philippine Duchesne, who brought the Society of the Sacred Heart to North America, visited the Academy twice, in 1822 and 1829. Katharine Drexel, founder of the Sisters of the Blessed Sacrament, visited the Sacred Heart Colored School on the grounds of the Academy in 1921. John Berchmans of the Jesuit order appeared in spirit to Mary Wilson on the second floor of the Academy in the Miracle of Grand Coteau in 1866. Cornelia Connelly, founder of the Society of the Holy Child Jesus, lived in a cottage on the grounds of the Academy from 1838 to 1842.

Chapter Eight

A Convergence of Saints

Throughout its history as a center for spiritual retreats and Catholic education, the holy ground of Grand Coteau has attracted countless people of deep faith and fervent prayer, including some who have risen to the level of sainthood.

Three formally declared saints and two other people en route to sainthood spent time in Grand Coteau or otherwise made significant contributions to the community, particularly in the area of education.

This convergence of saints and saintly people in this rural community is a testament to the idea that Grand Coteau is, indeed, a chosen place, a holy place.

The children of doctors and lawyers, as well as the sons and daughters of slaves, have benefited at the hands of four of these holy people – all women – whose lives were dedicated to the academic and religious education of young people.

Rose Philippine Duchesne, who brought the Society of the Religious of the Sacred Heart from France to North America in the early 1800s, visited the fledgling Academy of the Sacred Heart at Grand Coteau on two occasions, in 1822, the year after it was founded, and again in 1829.

Her visits were to check on the progress of the new academy and to lend moral support to her sisters, who were not having an easy time of it as they struggled to establish a school for girls in the untamed reaches of southern Louisiana.

Mother Duchesne, as she was called at the time, founded the first Sacred Heart school in America in St. Charles, Missouri, in 1818. To get to Grand Coteau, an

Rose Philippine Duchesne
Society of the Religious of the Sacred Heart

arduous three-week journey, she would board a steamboat at St. Louis, travel down the Mississippi River to Plaquemine, Louisiana, then make her way westward via flatboat, stagecoach and horseback.

She contracted yellow fever and nearly died on one of her trips. But she got over it. Mother Duchesne was a rugged, determined apostle of Christ who endured the rigors of frontier life to establish her schools and spread the Gospel to a part of the world that was badly in need of evangelization. Without complaint, she endured privations and hardships galore – floods, storms, disease, various hostilities and financial crises – and succeeded in her mission in a resounding fashion.

Shortly after Philippine Duchesne's death in 1852, Mother Anna du Rousier, who had great respect for Mother Duchesne's dedication, said she was thought of as a saint on earth, a holy woman whose canonization was a foregone conclusion. She quotes Msgr. Peter Richard Kenrick, Archbishop of St. Louis, as saying Mother Duchesne was "the noblest and most virtuous soul [I] had ever known." The shrine of St. Philippine Duchesne, who was canonized in 1988, is located on the campus of the Academy of the Sacred Heart in St. Charles, Missouri, and is open to the public.

Katharine Drexel, founder of the Sisters of the Blessed Sacrament for Indians and Colored People, donated funds on numerous occasions to help build, repair or renovate schools for black children in the Grand Coteau area. Responding to requests from Jesuit priests living at St. Charles College in Grand Coteau in the early part of the twentieth century, she sent various sums of money to support most any worthwhile effort that helped in the process of educating minority children.

In February of 1921 Mother Katharine visited the Sacred Heart Colored School on the grounds of the Academy of the Sacred Heart. She commended the nuns for their progressive educational program on behalf of minority children – a program that had been in operation for nearly half a century. She encouraged them to continue their efforts to provide a Catholic education for black children of the Grand Coteau area.

Mother Katharine (1858-1955) received millions of dollars from the trust fund set up by her father, a Philadelphia banker and philanthropist, and she spent all of it, and more, as she opened some sixty schools and missions for blacks and Indians, primarily in the Southern and Southwestern United States. In Louisiana alone, she and/or her congregation opened fourteen such institutions, half a dozen of which were within fifteen miles of Grand Coteau.

Katharine Drexel
Sisters of the Blessed Sacrament

So extensive was her influence in this part of the country that she is considered by some to be "The Patron Saint of South Louisiana." She also founded Xavier University in New Orleans.

Her complete dedication to the well-being of minority people is reflected in the fact that she made a fourth vow – in addition to the standard vows of poverty, chastity and obedience – when she began her religious congregation. She promised "to be the mother and servant of the Indian and Negro races and not to undertake any work which would lead to the neglect and abandonment of the Indian and Colored races."

In October of 2000, Pope John Paul II declared Katharine Drexel to be a saint, praising her for her profound compassion and spirit of generosity toward America's downtrodden minorities in the first half of the twentieth century.

"Katharine Drexel is an excellent example of that practical charity and generous solidarity with the less fortunate which has long been the distinguishing mark of American Catholics," the Pope stated. "May her example help young people in particular to appreciate that no greater treasure can be found in this world than in

John Berchmans
Society of Jesus

following Christ with an undivided heart and in using generously the gifts we have received for the service of others and for the building of a more just and fraternal world."

John Berchmans, who was studying to be a Jesuit priest in Rome at the time of his death in 1621, appeared in a vision in 1866 in the Academy of the Sacred Heart and was instrumental in the famous Miracle of Grand Coteau.

Mary Wilson, a postulant seeking to become a Sacred Heart nun, was dying from a painful and debilitating illness. John Berchmans appeared to her, told her he had been sent by God, and touched her. She was cured, totally and instantaneously.

It was the first authenticated miracle in North America and the third attributed to John Berchmans' intercession, and it led to his canonization in 1888.

Some years after this well-documented supernatural occurrence, a shrine to St. John Berchmans was built in the same room in which he appeared to Mary Wilson, on the second floor of the Academy. The shrine is open to the public by prior appointment.

Cornelia Connelly, founder of an order of teaching sisters called the Society of the Holy Child Jesus, lived in a cottage on the grounds of the Academy of the Sacred Heart from 1838 to 1842. While there she was the music instructor for the Academy, teaching piano and guitar. Her husband, Pierce Connelly, taught with the Jesuits at St. Charles College.

Both Cornelia and Pierce were from Philadelphia and had converted to Catholicism after having been members of the Episcopal Church. Pierce had been an Episcopal clergyman.

While living near the Academy, Cornelia prayed with the nuns, attended Mass regularly and grew in her faith. Under the tutelage of a Jesuit retreat director, she made the Spiritual Exercises of St. Ignatius in December of 1839 and subsequently resolved to turn over her life to the will of God. She prayed frequently and deeply to know God's will for her.

As a mother and a wife, she experienced more than her share of life's burdens. She wept over the deaths of her two-month-old daughter and her two-year-old son in the same year. Shortly thereafter her husband announced he wanted to sacrifice their marriage to become a Catholic priest. She was pregnant with their fifth child at the time.

Cornelia gave Pierce the chance to change his mind, but he stuck with his decision and left her in 1842.

Cornelia Connelly
Society of the Holy Child Jesus

She entered the Sacred Heart convent in Rome but was not happy with the monastic style of religious life she found there. She felt she was better suited to life in an apostolic order, one that was more in touch with the outside world. Mother Sophie Barat, founder of the Society of the Sacred Heart, agreed with her. Pope Gregory agreed with her, too, and urged her to establish a new religious order that would help to meet England's growing need for Catholic education.

Cornelia took the advice of the Pope and began formulating plans for a teaching order based on the spiritual works of mercy – instructing the ignorant, counseling the doubtful, etc. She decided to name her order the Society of the Holy Child Jesus. Her reasoning is explained in a brief biography published by her order:

"Her meditations led her to see the Incarnation as the highest expression of God's mercy and love. His gift of himself – emptied of all his glory, in the form of a little child, poor, humble, obedient for our sakes – was to be the model on which her followers would form themselves."

Cornelia took her vows in 1847 and became the superior of the new order. The first school opened in 1846 at Derby, England, serving English Catholics and Irish

Henriette Delille
Sisters of the Holy Family

immigrants. The order grew as schools were opened in various communities in England, as well as in France and the United States, and later in Africa and Latin America.

Meanwhile, Mother Connelly's former husband had dropped out of the priesthood and was waging a highly emotional though futile campaign to have his marriage reinstated and his family reunited. She was greatly distracted and humiliated by Pierce's antics, which included fruitless legal action, but she continued to do the work she felt God had called her to do.

Mother Connelly remained in England the rest of her life, faithful to her vocation as the founder and leader of the Society of the Holy Child Jesus. She died in 1879 at the age of 70. Her cause for canonization to sainthood was introduced in 1959; the Church declared her "venerable" in 1992.

Henriette Delille is the founder of a congregation of teaching sisters called the Sisters of the Holy Family. A free woman of color in antebellum New Orleans, Mother Delille and her sisters taught the sons and daughters of slaves in the Crescent City in the nineteenth century, and her congregation educated latter-day descendants of slaves in Grand Coteau in the twentieth century.

These Sisters of the Holy Family taught at St. Peter Claver School in Grand Coteau from 1947 until 1975; they took over the teaching duties from the Religious of the Sacred Heart, who, in turn, had been providing at least the rudiments of Catholic education to slaves since well before the Civil War.

Founded in 1842, Mother Delille's congregation ministered to the dying, the sick and the elderly, and they taught catechism to slaves and free people of color. The congregation began as a confraternity of lay women of African descent who banded together for their own spiritual growth, as well as to serve the city's most needy.

Henriette Delille was revered by those who knew of her good deeds and her faith-filled life. Her obituary noted:

"The crowd gathered for her funeral testified by its sorrow how keenly felt was the loss of her who, for the love of Jesus Christ, had made herself the humble servant of slaves."

She was given the title "Servant of God" by the Catholic Church in 1989 as the Church received her cause for canonization to sainthood and began the process of carefully studying her life and her prodigious works of mercy toward her poor and suffering neighbors.

In addition to these five saints and saints-to-be, how many more saints – unbeknown to anyone but God – have been strongly connected to the holy ground of Grand Coteau?

Of the hundreds of Jesuit novices and Sacred Heart novices who studied and trained in the novitiates at Grand Coteau, how many led such prayerful and virtuous lives that they are now, without question, among the saints in heaven?

How many men and women on retreat at St. Charles College or Our Lady of the Oaks have come to know God in a way that has changed their lives profoundly and set them on a path to true holiness?

If a saint, by one definition, is simply a person who has attained eternal salvation, then there are surely many more saints who have dwelled here, other than the ones who are widely known. For Grand Coteau is a place that is conducive to the making of saints. It is a holy place, where the Supreme Being reigns supreme, and where prayer and worship are the order of the day.

Fr. Cornelius
Thensted, S.J.
(1903-1981)

The Thensted Outreach Center in Grand Coteau occupies the building that was St. Peter Claver High, a Catholic school for blacks that operated from 1947 to 1977.

Chapter Nine

Fr. Thensted, Sr. Mike And The Second Great Commandment

One of the scribes came up, and ... decided to ask (Jesus), "Which is the first of all the commandments?" Jesus replied: "This is the first: 'Hear, O Israel! The Lord our God is Lord alone! Therefore you shall love the Lord your God with all your heart, with all your soul, with all your mind, and with all your strength.' This is the second: 'You shall love your neighbor as yourself.' There is no other commandment greater than these." (Mark 12:28-31).

ON THE MUCH-TRAVELED LITTLE COUNTRY ROAD THAT connects downtown Grand Coteau with the Academy of the Sacred Heart sits an inconspicuous two-story red brick building that was once known as St. Peter Claver High School. This Catholic school for blacks, whose roots go back to the nineteenth century, was closed in 1977 and re-opened five years later as the Thensted Outreach Center. The center is named in honor of a man of heroic virtue, a Jesuit priest who truly may be one of the undeclared saints of the twentieth century.

Fr. Cornelius J. Thensted worked in Grand Coteau and in nearby Bellevue for more than a quarter of a century. He was a fixture here, universally recognized as a true friend of the black community. He was, as one of his former parishioners described him, "an icon of social justice."

Fr. Thensted arrived in Grand Coteau in 1936 to begin his life's work of uplifting the people of the black community – spiritually, economically and educationally. He was 34 years old. He came as assistant pastor to Fr. Julius Oberholzer, S.J., who was pastor of St. Peter Claver Church, later to be known as Christ the King Church.

Cornelius Thensted was born in New Orleans on August 13, 1903. He graduated from Jesuit High School in 1920, attended Loyola University in New Orleans for a couple of years, then entered the Jesuit novitiate at Grand Coteau in 1924. After taking his vows in 1926 he studied at St. Michael's College in Spokane, Washington, taught chemistry at Spring Hill College in Mobile, Alabama, and studied theology at St. Mary's College in Kansas. He was ordained in 1935, did a tertianship in Cleveland, Ohio, then headed back to Grand Coteau.

Somewhere along the line, possibly while at Jesuit High or Loyola or while in

the novitiate, he realized the extent and the impact of the social injustice inherent in the racially segregated South. He felt great compassion for black people, who were victims of a racial and economic system that severely limited their educational and economic opportunity primarily, if not completely, because of the color of their skin. This was a system that sent black people to the back seats of the buses, to the balconies of movie theaters, to the back pews of the churches, and to the "Colored Entrance" of the restaurants and cafes. It was a cruel system with a discouraging message – if not a psychologically crippling one – that tended to crush the self-esteem and extinguish any flicker of hope for a better life.

When Fr. Thensted reported for duty in Grand Coteau he learned first-hand of the widespread poverty and lack of economic opportunity faced by blacks in this rural

Fr. Cornelius Thensted, S. J., visits with some of the children he helped educate in Grand Coteau, circa 1940. He was a fierce defender of the dignity and civil rights of the black community, working tirelessly for their best interests for more than a quarter of a century.

area of south Louisiana. It was not unlike the situation in much of the Southern United States. Like many poor white people, blacks were stuck in the country and on the small farms, some working as sharecroppers and getting deeper in debt as the years went by.

However, the Grand Coteau area was somewhat different from much of the rural South in terms of educational opportunity. The main reason for this was that the Religious of the Sacred Heart had been actively reaching out to educate black children since even before the Civil War, and they were continuing to do so when Fr. Thensted arrived in town. The school that had been opened formally in 1875, called Sacred Heart Colored School, was now named St. Peter Claver School and boasted a population of some 250 children from grades one through seven. The school was located on the grounds of the Academy of the Sacred Heart and would be moved, in 1939, to the grounds next to St. Peter Claver Church in downtown Grand Coteau. Children came from miles around, on foot, to go to school here. While some parents kept their youngsters home to work on the farms, others made their children go to school, at least for a few years, feeling that education just might be their means to a better life.

When Fr. Thensted began his work in Grand Coteau there were two separate Catholic churches in town: the white church, then called Sacred Heart and later to be named St. Charles Borromeo Church; and the black church, then called St. Peter Claver Church and later to be named Christ the King. He was assigned to the latter, which served the black people not only of Grand Coteau but also of the nearby communities of Sunset, Bellevue, Arnaudville and Prairie Basse. St. Peter Claver Church was housed in a wooden building that had been used as an auditorium at nearby St. Charles College.

Church attendance was fair but not near what it should be, in Fr. Thensted's estimation. He looked into the situation and soon learned that many blacks simply couldn't get to church regularly because they lived too far away to walk. Some came on horseback or in buggies or on bicycles, but none had cars. Besides, there was but one paved road in the area, and the dirt roads leading to it were made impassable when it rained, which was frequently.

This situation was remedied in part by the establishment of a little mission church and school in the rural community of Bellevue, approximately four miles northwest of Grand Coteau. An isolated mission situated among the cotton fields and sweet potato fields, it had been established sometime in the 1920s by the Jesuits in an effort to bring the rudiments of secular education and religious instruction to people who didn't have the means to travel even to Grand Coteau. The little school was but three or four rooms, and the pupils were instructed by a few lay teachers who lived a short distance from the school. Catechism was taught twice a week by Jesuit scholastics who came from the novitiate in Grand Coteau.

The Bellevue Mission was Fr. Thensted's initial assignment when he came to the Grand Coteau area, his primary responsibility for the first four years of his tenure. One of his first initiatives was to organize religious retreats for black adults, based, of course, on the Spiritual Exercises of St. Ignatius. The first retreats, one for men and one for women, were held in a public school building located in the community, with about 300 men and 300 women in attendance. He celebrated an open air Mass during the men's retreat, and some 700 people attended.

Seeing the great need for basic education and religious instruction, Fr. Thensted envisioned Bellevue as a more vibrant community, with a larger Catholic school, many more pupils, and a bigger church with greater attendance. Toward this end, he requested that the Sisters of the Holy Family, who were based in New Orleans, send some of their sisters to teach in the school and to live in Bellevue. The superior of the congregation agreed and sent four sisters to begin teaching in the 1942-43 school year. A nearby house was moved onto the school property and renovated into a modest convent for the sisters.

For the next decade and more Fr. Thensted continued working to build up the Bellevue complex. In 1949 he had the church enlarged and bricked; in 1950 and '51 he had a gymnasium and cafeteria built and the school enlarged to accommodate some 300 or more children; and in 1952 he had a new, larger convent constructed.

Working in partnership with him for much of this period was Sister Jane Frances Evans, who came to Bellevue as the school's first principal and served in this capacity for a total of thirty-five years. She went way beyond the traditional roles of principal and classroom teacher, demanding that local farmers allow their children to attend school, convincing the local School Board to provide bus service for her students, and helping to organize the events that provided much of the funding to operate her school.

"The people loved and respected both Sr. Jane Frances and Fr. Thensted because they gave the people access to a better life – spiritually, economically and educationally," says Sr. Eva Regina Martin, a Sister of the Holy Family who was reared in Grand Coteau.

Christ the King Church in Grand Coteau was built in the early 1940s to serve black Catholics of the area. The new structure, which replaced the old wooden St. Peter Claver Church, is now known as St. Charles Chapel. **Below:** *Celebrants and attendees gathered for a picture following a special Mass and dedication ceremony in September of 1942.* **Right:** *The special Mass was filled to overflowing, as were many of the Masses in the church's heyday.*

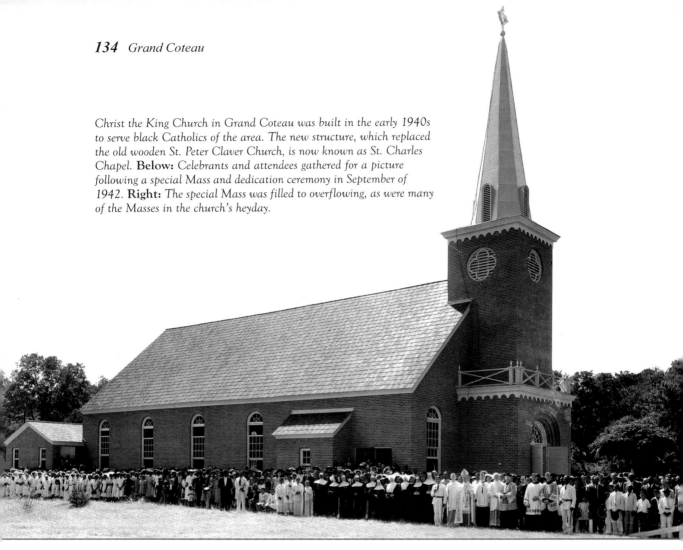

After working almost exclusively in Bellevue for four years, Fr. Thensted was named pastor of St. Peter Claver Church in 1941, taking over from Fr. Oberholzer. So, in addition to continuing to improve the Bellevue Mission, he launched a program to expand the church-and-school complex in Grand Coteau. In 1947 he built a new St. Peter Claver School and had the old one remodeled and converted to a convent for the Sisters of the Holy Family. As was the case at Bellevue, he convinced the Sisters of the Holy Family to staff St. Peter Claver School. The need for teaching staff was created when the Religious of the Sacred Heart – who had staffed the school for some seventy-three years – withdrew because their order was moving toward a stricter application of the rules of cloister, thus reducing the time they could spend away from their convent.

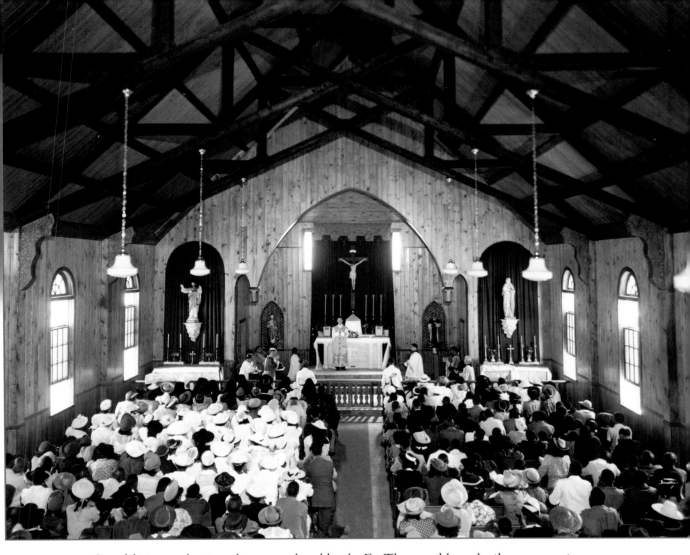

In addition to having the new school built, Fr. Thensted later built a gymnasium and a separate elementary school. Earlier, he had played a major role in the building of a new brick church, called Christ the King Church, which was erected next to the school in 1942.

The buildup of the complexes at Grand Coteau and Bellevue were the work of an extraordinarily energetic and devoted man, a person who was driven. He was completely dedicated to uplifting an impoverished minority who had endured privations of every kind for generations. Cornelius Thensted was the quintessential mover and shaker. Many who knew him called him "Stepper," because he was always steppin', always movin', almost running as he went quickly from place to place, task to task. He was a tall and slender man who remained thin because of his methodical fasting, his modest eating habits, and his constant activity. He was up at 3:30 or 4 in the morning to pray and meditate, celebrate the Mass, and get moving on one project or another that would improve the spiritual and/or material well-being of the black people of the Grand Coteau area.

This brown-haired, brown-eyed Jesuit not only moved about quickly but he spoke loudly, very loudly. The volume of his voice was part of his booming persona. It sometimes frightened the children. It signaled adults that he was a man who meant business; even his detractors thought twice before getting in his way.

And he did have detractors: Not everyone in the area was comfortable with his progressive mind-set, with his projects and programs designed to unite and strengthen the black community.

One of his former acquaintances, Samuel Henry, now a deacon at St. Charles Borromeo Church, testifies to Fr. Thensted's aggressive, determined nature.

"Fr. Thensted was kind of rough. He didn't play around.... He got what he wanted; if he went after it, he got it," Deacon Henry says.

When Fr. Thensted first came to Grand Coteau he drove a motorcycle, scooting around the area at a rather high rate of speed. The motorcycle was loud and tended to awaken the Jesuits at St. Charles College, sometimes an hour before they were scheduled to rise, at 5 a.m. But Fr. Thensted had places to go, people to see, schools and churches to build. He worked long days, sometimes remaining in his office, on the grounds of the St. Peter Claver complex, until 10:30 or 11 at night.

After he had been in Grand Coteau for a number of years, he acquired a car. He drove the car at a speed that was appropriate to his pace of life, i.e., over the speed limit.

While he conformed to the dress code for Jesuit priests, there was a twist to the way he wore his clothes: He would tuck his cassock into his belt to allow greater freedom of movement when he walked, i.e., so he could walk faster. He also wore rubber boots, to get through the mud that seemed to be everywhere in this rural area, even after a modest rain.

Fr. Thensted was a deeply religious and spiritual man who spent many of his waking hours in prayer of one form or another. His love of the Mass and his devotion to the Blessed Sacrament and to the Rosary were well known in the community. Fr. Thomas Jenniskens, who knew Fr. Thensted well, having been in the novitiate when Fr. Thensted was pastor of St. Peter Claver Church, recalls that Fr. Thensted would attend Mass as many times as he could in a given day. He consistently organized retreats for his parishioners throughout his tenure in Grand Coteau and Bellevue, always including a Mass as the high point of the retreat. He seldom passed the grotto of Our Lady of Lourdes – which was located near the rectory, where he lived – without stopping to pray, at least for a little while. Even when he was very busy in his church office he would stop in the afternoon, go into the church with his staff and pray the Rosary. He also made time to teach religion at St. Peter Claver High School and to visit the children in the lower grades.

The students understood generally that Fr. Thensted was a friend of the black community, but still many of them were afraid of him. He was loud and strict and seemed so tall. When students misbehaved, he'd make them kneel in the corner of the class. He demanded that they learn their catechism, that they say their prayers without clowning around, and that they behave respectfully during the weekly school Mass. And woe to those who crossed him.

Ironically, though, to those who knew him well and understood his motives, Fr. Thensted was the kindest of souls.

"Fr. Thensted was gruff-sounding," Fr. Jenniskens recalls. "He didn't sound like a gentleman, but he truly was a gentle man."

Fr. Thensted had a tendency to give advice on marriage and all sorts of subjects, some of it unsolicited. When he would hear of a married couple who were seriously considering separating, he would go to their house, invited or not, and counsel them to calm down, try to work things out, and remain together. He succeeded in some of these interventions and not in others.

Fr. Thensted sometimes engaged in lively discussion with the novices and juniors at St. Charles College, including his friend, Fr. Jenniskens, on subjects such as the value of religious study as compared with religious practice. He felt study was very useful up to a point, but he, for one, was glad to be finished with the classroom and out in the world, practicing his faith.

One way he practiced his faith was through daily acts of compassion and understanding toward his parishioners, young and old. On numerous occasions he secured financial aid, jobs or scholarships for bright students who wanted to continue their education past the seventh grade, which was the last grade for Southern rural schools in those days.

For instance, he helped a girl named Mary Murray by getting her a scholarship to a top-quality Catholic girls' boarding school, Holy Rosary Institute in nearby Lafayette. One of sixteen children, Mary finished as valedictorian of her class in 1943, went on to graduate from Xavier University in New Orleans in 1947, then returned to Grand Coteau to teach elementary grades at St. Peter Claver School for some thirty years. She was elected mayor of Grand Coteau in 1991 and served till 1998.

In another instance, Fr. Thensted discovered that one of the men cooking in the Jesuit novitiate, Matthew Ozene, was an especially bright and conversant fellow who could be and should be in a more challenging line of work. So, Fr. Thensted stepped in to try to help him improve his lot in life. Mr. Ozene's daughter, Pauline Ozene Edmond of Grand Coteau, says she will be grateful always for the helping hand her dad received.

"Fr. Thensted told my daddy he was too smart to be in the kitchen cooking, so he arranged for him to get an education at St. Emma's in Rock Castle, Virginia," she says, referring to the trade school for blacks where her father was trained to be a master carpenter.

While Fr. Thensted helped dozens of his parishioners get the education they couldn't afford on their own, perhaps an even more intricate financial feat was the manner in which he – along with a small army of volunteers – raised the money to fund the building projects at Bellevue and Grand Coteau.

Fr. Thensted believed completely in the Biblical injunction, "Ask, and you shall receive." He was not shy about asking or even begging, for he was deeply, deeply motivated by the cries of the poor and the bottomless pit of need which he saw all around him. There seemed to be no doubt in his mind, or in his heart, that this was one of the things the Lord was calling him to do, so he did it joyfully and with as much persistence and imagination as he could muster.

First, he enlisted the aid of his parishioners to volunteer to put together church bazaars, cake sales, raffles, barbecues and various other fund-raising events. The annual bazaars at Bellevue are said to have raised tens of thousands of dollars on a single weekend. All sorts of jobs at the church complexes at Bellevue and Grand Coteau – from carpentry, to painting, to yard work, to office work – were done on a volunteer basis. The black community felt a strong sense of ownership of the facilities in both Grand Coteau and Bellevue. This community spirit – which blossomed under Fr. Thensted's leadership – generated a high level of cooperation that had scores of people pitching in to get things done.

One of his most innovative fund-raising projects was the publication of a newsletter titled "Please...," which solicited donations of every kind to help the people and the parish of Christ the King. The newsletter was mailed three or four times a year to 2,000 to 3,000 people all over the United States who were made aware of

Fr. Cornelius Thensted, S.J., poses with his staff and volunteers who helped publish and mail the "Please..." newsletter in the 1950s. The newsletter was effective in raising money to help fund several projects that benefited the local black community. In the background are rows of files containing the names and addresses of the thousands of people to whom the newsletter was sent. Left to right are Eva Martin, Mary Murray, Catharine Carson, Germaine Coco and Fr. Thensted.

the needs of Fr. Thensted's parish on an on-going basis. Many of the names on the mailing list were people known by Fr. Thensted, while others were gathered from myriad sources. In addition to appealing for donations, the newsletter reported on the religious and educational activities of the parishioners, gave an informal accounting of how the donations were being used, and thanked the donors. The newsletter was printed in the church office then addressed and folded by student volunteers before being mailed. The results of these direct mail campaigns were most gratifying to Fr. Thensted, for they produced a steady stream of money as well as clothing, furniture and even jewelry. Much of the money was set aside in a building fund, while the goods were distributed to the needy through a makeshift thrift store, called "The Box."

He also appealed successfully to Mother Katharine Drexel, founder of the Sisters of the Blessed Sacrament for Indians and Colored People. Mother Katharine, an heiress to a fortune left by her father, a Philadelphia banker, was in the process of opening some sixty schools around the Southern and Southwestern United States for underprivileged minorities, including about a dozen in south Louisiana. Fr. Thensted felt he could count on her for financial help, inasmuch as they were kindred spirits in their commitment to helping the poor. A series of letters was exchanged between them in 1938 and 1939. Her letters usually contained checks to help with teachers' salaries or building projects, while his asked for financial aid or bore words of gratitude. One of his letters to her, dated December 8, 1939, states:

> Thank you for your check towards the teachers' salary.... Your letter this month was more than welcome. Because it arrived a little late, I could not help thinking how hard it would be to make ends meet if the check did not come.... A great weight was taken off my mind.

In an earlier letter to Mother Katharine, dated May 11, 1939, Fr. Thensted's deep gratitude, and his humility, are manifested as he thanks her for another monetary gift:

> May the Sacred Heart and Our Blessed Mother reward your generous charity!
> You can count on my prayers and a daily remembrance at the altar of sacrifice, but the prayers of our little ones, "Christ's least brethren," will be more powerful than mine, and each day at school they will pray for you and your Community.
> I cannot write more than "thank you," but He who knows what my heart feels for you at your kindness towards my mission will best communicate it to you.

If Fr. Thensted was eloquent and sincere in his letters of gratitude to Mother Katharine, he was equally so in the letters he wrote to those on his regular mailing list as he appealed for funds. In a December of 1957 letter soliciting urgently needed financial help for his people, he wrote:

> ...You have helped us to conduct our two schools to bring religion into the lives of our Negro children. For this we are most grateful. But much more remains to be done....
> So I come to you again. This time I am not merely asking, I am not only begging, but in the name of the Lord, I am pleading with you to continue to help us with alms and even to interest others in our work for the temporal and eternal welfare of our Negro children and of those who will be influenced by their lives.

A major donor who played a significant role in the on-going campaigns to fund Fr. Thensted's projects was Madame Theresa Bajat Chatrian, a wealthy resident of Grand Coteau whose husband had moved here from France. She was like a second mother to Fr. Thensted and had him over for meals frequently. Among other gifts, she bought him a car to replace his motorcycle and paid his way for a trip to Rome. On several occasions when one of Fr. Thensted's fund-raising drives fell short, she would write a check for the balance needed to reach the goal. She was grateful that God had blessed her with an abundance of material wealth, and she gladly shared it with those in need. She seemed to have complete trust in Fr. Thensted and the worthiness of the causes which he championed. She also donated occasionally to projects associated with the Jesuit novitiate.

While Fr. Thensted did literally everything he could to raise money on behalf of the black community, he was equally as resolute that no harm should come to any of the people in his care. He vigorously defended the dignity and aspirations of his parishioners, taking on all challengers. He was like a father defending his house from intruders, like a mother bear protecting her young. While it is true that he would discipline children for misbehaving, and he would lecture adults who were going astray, he did so in love, and with the best motives.

But not everyone who took his people to task did so in the same spirit. Some were simply prejudiced against blacks for no logical reason, acting out of cruelty, ignorance or fear.

In 1943, two years after becoming pastor of the black church in Grand Coteau, Fr. Thensted received an unwelcome visit from two town officials. They told him they wanted him to cut back on the number of activities he was organizing for his parishioners, particularly nighttime events such as socials, dances and even religious functions. There was something about black people getting together at night that made some of the local white population nervous, insecure, the town officials explained. Fr. Thensted was outraged. His blood began to boil and his already-loud voice became even louder. No, he would not listen to reason, because what the officials were proposing was unreasonable and mean-spirited. He ran them out of his office and never heard from them again on this subject.

Some years later, in 1952, Fr. Thensted hired a secretary named Catharine Carson, a woman of 27 from Ohio who had been wanting to move to the South and work in some capacity for a black parish. Her intention was to work as an unpaid volunteer for a year, so long as her room and board were paid. However, she ended up working as a volunteer for five years, living free of charge in a cottage on the grounds of the Academy of the Sacred Heart. After that, she began receiving a modest salary, and she stayed another thirty years. The level of job satisfaction was high enough to keep her interested and involved for all this time. She felt that the work she was doing was important, that the cause for which she was working was noble, and that the employer whom she served was a just and honorable man.

Miss Carson was an efficient secretary who handled a large amount of clerical work, thus freeing Fr. Thensted from much of the details that kept him bogged down in the office. He was very pleased that she had come; her presence freed him to go out and do his spiritual work.

In addition to her office work, she helped with various church functions, such as dances, socials, picnics and the like. However, something about her being the only white woman at these functions was disturbing to some of the white community. Apparently, in their minds, it amounted to "mixing of the races," which was taboo at this time in the Deep South. So, a petition was circulated and signatures obtained asking her to leave town. One day, when Fr. Thensted was out of town, a sheriff's deputy came to the office, served Miss Carson with the petition, and told her she'd have to go. At first, she was scared, then she was hurt to see the names of the people who had signed, then she was angry.

Not surprisingly, so was Fr. Thensted when he returned the next day and learned what had happened. He stormed out of the office, tracked down the instigator of the petition, and stated loudly that his secretary wasn't going anywhere.

It was obvious to Fr. Thensted that quite a few of the white population disapproved of his efforts to uplift the black community, and while they didn't have the nerve to confront him on the subject, they were trying to undermine his efforts by intimidating his support staff. He thought it was cowardly, and he said so.

On another occasion in the 1950s Fr. Thensted was riding in the cab of a pickup truck with two of his parishioners, a black man and his daughter. The bed of the truck was piled high with furniture and bags of clothing, which had been gathered from a collection station in New Orleans, i.e., Fr. Thensted's sister's garage. The goods were being hauled back to Grand Coteau to be distributed to families in need. A policeman stopped the truck, and the black man got out to talk to him. The discussion became a bit heated, and when Fr. Thensted heard something about "going to jail," he emerged from the truck and approached the policeman.

"What's the problem, officer?" he asked in a gruff, authoritarian tone.

The policeman seemed surprised to see a white man get out of the truck.

"No problem, Father," he said, as he spotted the priest's Roman collar. "The load is a little high, that's all. Y'all be careful driving home."

The policeman got back in his car and drove off.

The young girl in the truck that day was Jean Jones. She grew up to be Jean Jones Coco, Mayor of Grand Coteau. She says she remembers every detail of the incident on the road from New Orleans, and she admires Fr. Thensted and what he did for her people on a regular basis.

"Fr. Thensted portrayed himself as rugged, but he had a tender, loving heart," she observes. "I'd say he actually loved us, the black people of Grand Coteau."

It would be safe to conclude that Fr. Thensted loved all of the human family, for he was clearly a moral person, even a holy man. He knew that the Second Great Commandment – "Love thy neighbor as thyself" – was spoken plainly, without equivocation, without regard to race, color or creed. He understood that it was, and is, and always will be the second pillar upon which all moral law rests.

Fr. Thensted served continuously in Grand Coteau and Bellevue from 1936 to 1965, except for an assignment in Tampa, Florida, from 1958 to 1960. By age 62, in 1965, Fr. Thensted was worn out. He had given everything he had to the God he served and the people he embraced. His health was declining; his step was slowing down.

He would be moved to positions that did not require so much of him. He be-came an assistant pastor of a church in Mobile for a few years, then one in Tampa, then one in New Orleans.

In 1975 he retired to Grand Coteau to live with his fellow Jesuits at St. Charles College, seemingly unable to perform his priestly duties. The spring in his step was now gone, as was the light in his eyes. He had even become soft-spoken. It seemed that his days of doing great things were over.

Sr. Margaret "Mike" Hoffman, a member of the Religious of the Sacred Heart, founded the Thensted Center in an effort to continue Fr. Cornelius Thensted's work of uplifting and supporting the black community in the Grand Coteau area.

*   *   *   *   *

Sister Margaret Hoffman, a Religious of the Sacred Heart, also known as "Sister Mike," arrived in Grand Coteau in 1975, the same year in which Fr. Thensted returned. Her mission was not unlike the mission that Fr. Thensted had pursued here in an earlier time: working for the spiritual, physical and economic well-being of the black community.

Sr. Mike was in Grand Coteau at the direction of her superior, Mother Rita Karam, the provincial of the Southern Province. Mother Karam, who had previously taught at the Academy of the Sacred Heart in Grand Coteau and who was a native of south Louisiana, had said to Sr. Mike:

"There is so much need among the people who live there, so much poverty. And we have been there for so long. Go and see how you can help them."

Being not only a religious sister but also a registered nurse, Sr. Mike had spent most of her adult life ministering to the aged and the infirm. She had worked for many years in homes for the aged, in cities such as Detroit, St. Louis and Kenosha, Wisconsin. Her latest assignment had been working in a nursing home, caring for elderly members of her own order, in St. Charles, Missouri.

Now, in Grand Coteau, she would provide home health care for the elderly and infirm and deliver meals-on-wheels, as well as working nights at University Medical Center in nearby Lafayette. She would also visit and help care for elderly and sick Jesuits in the infirmary at St. Charles College.

One of those Jesuits was Fr. Thensted. He seemed to be suffering from what is known today as Alzheimer's. The infirmary staff were concerned about his wandering off. He was sometimes found in the Jesuits' dairy barn, sometimes gathering bottles from the ditches around town, and too often walking on the highway that ran in front of the college. He didn't recognize people he had known for years. Sometimes he would forget his own name.

Sr. Mike learned of Fr. Thensted's work not from him but from his fellow Jesuits and from conversations with members of the black community. The more she learned, the more impressed she became. This good-hearted man had given his life in service to the poor, building schools and churches, raising hopes for a better future, promoting dignity and self-respect among the black community. He had secured scholarships, organized retreats and raised money, all the while praying humbly before the Lord and serving as an example of what it means to live the messages of the Gospels.

And, now, here he was, in the infirmary, his productive years seemingly behind him, his face drawn and ashen, his body bent over by age, staring out the window at the grounds he walked as a novice some forty years earlier. He looked small and helpless.

One cold morning in early January of 1977, Sr. Mike was driving her car to the Academy of the Sacred Heart to administer physical therapy to a religious sister who was recovering from a broken leg. She spotted Fr. Thensted walking on the side of the road, apparently headed for the Academy. So, she stopped to offer him a ride.

"Where you headed, Father?" she asked.

"I'm going to say Mass at the Academy," he said after a few moments of hesitation.

Sr. Mike was somewhat surprised by his response because she felt he wouldn't be capable of saying Mass, because of the state of his health.

"Well, hop in, I'll give you a ride," she said.

She drove him to the Academy, walked him to the Shrine of St. John Berchmans, on the second floor, and said good-bye. She then proceeded to another room on the same floor to work with her patient with the broken leg. A little while later she heard a commotion in the hall outside the room where the shrine is located.

One sister was complaining to another about Fr. Thensted's wanting to say Mass. Sr. Mike stepped into the hall to find out what was happening.

"What's going on?" she asked.

"Father says he's here to say Mass. He can't say Mass...," one sister responded.

"Yes, that's what he told me, too, that he was coming to say Mass," Sr. Mike said.

"I've prepared everything for the Mass, but I don't think he is able to say Mass," said one of the sisters, who was the sacristan. "Still, he insists he is going to do it. It's not right. I just put everything there on the altar, but I won't have anything more to do with it. I'm leaving."

Meanwhile, Fr. Thensted had managed to put on the proper vestments for Mass, and he was just standing there, at the altar, and staring straight ahead. Three sisters were kneeling in the pews, waiting for Mass to begin.

Fr. Thensted continued to stand there, obviously not knowing what to do. Moved to compassion by what she was seeing, Sr. Mike walked up to the altar and stood beside the silent priest. She opened the Mass book and gently touched the spot on the page where he was to begin. And he began.

"In the name of the Father, and of the Son, and of the Holy Spirit..."

He continued with the Mass, proceeding relatively well, all things considered, and when he would forget what to do, Sr. Mike would help him. It was as though the two of them were concelebrating the Mass.

The Mass proceeded to the consecration, to transubstantiation, and the glorious presence of Jesus. Sr. Mike could practically see the Risen Lord standing near the altar in all his magnificence: radiant, all-powerful, compassionate. She imagined Jesus placing an approving hand upon the shoulder of the ailing priest and saying to him, "Well done, my good and faithful servant," thus signaling that Fr. Thensted's work on earth was finished. At the same time, she felt a distinct movement in her soul, not a voice but a message that she was to take over Fr. Thensted's mission of service to the black community. It was an overwhelming feeling, a clear understanding that came to her. She came to the knowledge that this is something God wanted her to do, to continue the work Fr. Thensted had done so well and for so long. She accepted the mandate, vowing then and there, in the presence of the Lord, to carry on Fr. Thensted's work and to keep his memory alive.

When the Mass was over, Fr. Thensted took off his vestments in the sacristy, and Sr. Mike drove him back to St. Charles College.

For the next several years, an inspired Sr. Mike continued to provide home health care for the elderly of the Grand Coteau area, to care for those in the infirmary at St. Charles College, and to work nights at University Medical Center.

While working in the hospital she saw a number of surgeries performed on people who were sent home to recover after only a short time in the hospital. She wondered what happened to these people when they went home; she doubted that their families were given adequate instruction on how to care for the patients once they returned home. So, she followed up on the patients who lived in the Grand Coteau area and taught a number of families how to care for their loved ones after surgery, instructing them on things such as wound care, nutrition, and the rudiments of physical therapy.

She used the occasion of these home visits to find out from these families what they needed, how she might be able to help them further. Gradually, the people opened up to her, and she learned that they wanted a community center, a place they could go that would meet their various needs. It might offer after-school care, where children could play rather than running the streets. It might offer tutoring for young people and a reading program for older ones. It might continue to feature a meals-on-wheels program, as well as home health care services.

For several years Sr. Mike and a few of her fellow Religious of the Sacred Heart provided as many of these services as they could, though on a home-visit basis.

Meanwhile, in 1977, St. Peter Claver High School was closed due to dwindling enrollment and chronic financial problems. Over the next several years the building began to deteriorate due to neglect and vandalism.

In 1980 Sr. Mike obtained permission to clean and refurbish the place and to convert it to a community center to serve the underprivileged of Grand Coteau. Reflecting her desire to keep Fr. Thensted's memory alive, the place would be called the Thensted Outreach Center.

But there was much work to be done. So, she and several members of the community, headed by Peter Smith, a local professional builder who had served as the town's second black mayor, put in countless hours. They cleaned and scrubbed and patched. They replaced the broken windows, had the partially collapsed roof repaired, and painted till their arms and backs were tired.

Finally, after more than a year of work, the place was opened in 1982. Sr. Mike's programs had a major positive impact on the community. She was assisted by an exceptionally dedicated parishioner named Mrs. Fran Cochran and several Religious of the Sacred Heart. Sr. Mike directed the operation for a total of fifteen years then moved on to other assignments, in Uganda, New Orleans and California. The director's job was assumed eventually by Julia Richard, a 1971 graduate of St. Peter Claver High School. She continues to get the job done with the help of a few paid employees and three Religious of the Sacred Heart, who work as volunteers.

The services provided by the Thensted Center today include home visits to the elderly and shut-ins; a thrift store with clothing, furniture and household items; an emergency food pantry; after-school tutoring; individual and family counseling; regular get-togethers for seniors citizens; money-management and budgeting instructions; and career counseling.

So, the Thensted Center has turned out pretty much the way Sr. Mike envisioned it. The same Gospel values which Fr. Thensted believed in and lived by are practiced daily in the center that bears his name.

Fr. Thensted died the year before the center was opened, in the Jesuit retirement home in New Orleans on February 15, 1981, at age 77. He had been a member of the Society of Jesus for 57 years. He is buried in the Jesuit Cemetery behind St. Charles Borromeo Church in Grand Coteau.

The spirit of this exemplary Christian man, and those who labored with him, is evident today in Grand Coteau and the surrounding area. Their labor of love, their practice of the Second Great Commandment as a way of life, continues to contribute greatly to making Grand Coteau the holy place that it is.

Appendix 1

Silence

The silence of retreat is not simply a shutdown of communication with the outside world but rather a process of coming to stillness.

It is much like the case of the busy person caught up in the affairs of life and of work who went to the desert solitary and complained about frustration in prayer, flawed virtue and failed relationships. The hermit listened attentively to his visitor's rehearsal of the struggle and disappointments in leading the Christian life. He then went into the dark recesses of his cave and came out with a basin and pitcher of water. "Now watch the water as I pour it into the basin," he said. The water splashed on the bottom and against the sides of the container. It was agitated and turbulent. At first the stirred-up water swirled around the inside of the basin, but then it gradually began to settle until finally the small fast ripples gave way to larger swells that oscillated back and forth, and the surface became tranquil and calm, so smooth, in fact, that the visitor could see his face reflected in the placid water. "That is the way it is when you live in the midst of others," said the hermit. "You do not see yourself as you really are because of all the confusion and disturbance." Nor do you recognize the divine presence in your life, he might have added.

It takes time for the water to settle and become quiet; it is a process that one must wait upon, for attempts to hasten it are an interference that only stir up the water anew.

Retreat silence is both exterior and interior. Exterior silence precludes speaking with any person other than one's director and making loud noises that can disturb or distract others. It bespeaks reverence for God, whom alone one is intent upon hearing within, and for the solitude of others who are similarly waiting upon his voice. Exterior silence is a settling on the surface that must precede the deep interior stillness of prayer. Interior silence consists in tuning out that inner dialog with self that (can be) a jumble of frivolous thoughts, worrisome cares and negative feelings. The careful observance of silence can be frightening at first and easily lead to the temptation to seek diversion with self or with others before God has been able to make himself heard above the clatter that surrounds our minds and hearts. It is an exercise of faith and of hope, which seldom fails to result in that inner peace that is a sign of God's presence.

Silence is not an end in itself, an exercise in self-control for greater self-discipline, but a means to an end. The end is prayer. Prayer in the first place is a listening to God. If one is to hear him, then he or she must be free from whatever could distract from the sound of his voice. Silence establishes that necessary condition for hearing the Lord speak, for recognizing the personal love that he wants to reveal and the word of truth that he has to communicate.

A retreat is an extended period of prayer, a time to experience the transcendent Other and grow in intimacy with the Lord. However, one cannot get to know another personally and deeply unless the two spend time together alone. Silence is a way to make this solitude a reality. As Fr. Henri Nouwen puts it: "Silence is solitude practiced in action."

The hermit Arsenius, one of those great men… of prayer who lived in the Egyptian desert between the third and sixth centuries, once remarked, "I have often repented of having spoken but never of having remained silent." That is wise counsel for every disciple, but especially for every retreatant.

Source: Jesuit Spirituality Center, Grand Coteau, La.

Appendix 2

A Directed Retreat

Since 1972 the Jesuit Spirituality Center at St. Charles College in Grand Coteau, Louisiana, has been offering directed retreats to men and women of all faiths.

A directed retreat is an opportunity for an individual to focus on one's personal relationship with God, particularly one's prayer life, as well as one's relationship with others; this is done over a period of time in solitude and silence in communication with God. The length of time can extend from three to eight days to a full-length retreat of thirty days. The most commonly requested retreat is usually a five-day one.

During this time the retreatant meets daily with his/her director, a member of the staff of the Jesuit Spirituality Center. Normally, the director will allow periods of forty-five minutes for the retreatant, but this can be shortened or lengthened according to the needs of the retreatant. During the opening session with the director, the retreatant shares with the director information about his/her relationship with God and his/her prayer life. Such information helps the director in his or her role as the retreatant's spiritual companion. At this time the director will usually assign several scripture passages from the Old and/or New Testament for the individual to pray over prior to their next meeting on the following day.

At each subsequent meeting the retreatant is invited to share with the director his/her experiences in prayer, how God might have touched the retreatant, whether he/she felt consoled or depressed, whatever feelings or interior movements the individual might want to pass on to the director. It often happens that in trying to share and express one's own experience of God in prayer to another, that experience becomes clearer in one's own mind and heart. And this helps the director in suggesting suitable scripture passages that will meet the needs and desires of the retreatant.

How the retreatant prays the scripture passages during the course of the day is left up to the retreatant and the director. Usually three or four formal periods of prayer from a half to a full hour are recommended; the scheduling of these prayer periods is left up to the retreatant. Furthermore, individuals often spend time informally reflecting on their prayer experiences, looking to see where God has touched them and becoming more conscious of their inner feelings. For the most part the day should be one of relaxation and rest in the presence of God with little strain or pressure. Each person eventually finds his or her own daily rhythm of prayer, reflection and relaxation in an atmosphere of silence, peace and calm – all of which are essential to a directed retreat. The important thing is to be alone with God in a spirit of silence and simplicity, for it is in this climate that one can best experience the voice of God.

The only prerequisite for making a retreat is one's desire to spend time with God in silence and solitude (and the grounds at the Spirituality Center definitely lend themselves to this) and a willingness to share one's prayer experiences with the director. If one does not have a regular life of prayer, a directed retreat would be an aid to one who desires to get into a formal routine of prayer.

To help a retreatant to relax both spiritually and physically, the Center offers 900 acres of beautiful farmland interspersed with live oak, pine and pecan trees, azaleas and other flowering bushes in the heart of Cajun country. Bicycles, an outdoor swimming pool, and walking and jogging paths are available for exercising and relaxation.

For further information about a directed retreat, contact the Jesuit Spirituality Center at (337) 662-5251.

Source: Jesuit Spirituality Center, Grand Coteau, La.

Contact Information

To inquire about making a retreat at the Jesuit Spirituality Center...

Jesuit Spirituality Center
P.O. Box C
Grand Coteau, LA 70541
Website: home.centurytel.net/spiritualitycenter

Phone: (337) 662-5251
Fax: (337) 662-3187
E-mail: jespirtcen@centurytel.net

To inquire about making a retreat at Our Lady of the Oaks...

Our Lady of the Oaks Retreat House
P.O. Drawer D
Grand Coteau, LA 70541
Website: www.ourladyoftheoaks.com

Phone: (337) 662-5410
Fax: (337) 662-5331
E-mail: olorhgcla@centurytel.net

To inquire about becoming a member of the Society of the Sacred Heart...

Society of the Sacred Heart
United States Province
4389 W. Pine Blvd.
St. Louis, MO 63108

Phone: (314) 652-1500
Fax: (314) 534-6800
E-mail: provincialhouse@rscj.org
Website: www.rscj.org

To inquire about becoming a member of the Sisters of the Holy Family...

Sisters of the Holy Family
6901 Chef Menteur Hwy.
New Orleans, LA 70126
Website: www.sistersoftheholyfamily.org

Phone: (504) 241-5400
Fax: (504) 241-3957

To inquire about becoming a member of the Society of Jesus...

New Orleans Province
  of the Society of Jesus
Director of Vocations
500 S. Jefferson Davis Pkwy.
New Orleans, LA 70119

Phone: (504) 821-0334
Fax: (504) 822-5322
E-mail: noprovsj@norprov.org
Website: www.norprov.org

Sources

Books

Barry, Bonnie T. *For the Greater Honor and Glory of God: A History of the Building of St. Charles Borromeo Catholic Church.* Sunset, Louisiana, 1987.

Baudier, Roger. *The Catholic Church in Louisiana.* New Orleans: Archdiocese of New Orleans, 1939.

Brodrick, James, S.J. *The Origin of the Jesuits.* Chicago: Loyola Press, 1997.

Callan, Louise, RSCJ. *Philippine Duchesne: Frontier Missionary of the Sacred Heart* (Abridged Edition). Westminster, Maryland: The Newman Press, 1965.

——, *The Society of the Sacred Heart in North America.* London, New York, Toronto: Longmans, Green and Co., 1937.

Conrad, Glenn R. *Crevasse!: The 1927 Flood in Acadiana.* Lafayette, La.: Center for Louisiana Studies, 1994.

Dawes, Dorothy and Nolan, Charles. *Religious Pioneers: Building the Faith in the Archdiocese of New Orleans.* New Orleans: Archdiocese of New Orleans, 2004.

Fleming, Fr. David, S.J. *Draw Me Into Your Friendship: The Spiritual Exercises – A Literal Translation and a Contemporary Reading.* St. Louis: Institute of Jesuit Resources, 1996.

Jurado, Manuel Ruiz, S.J. *For the Greater Glory of God: A Spiritual Retreat with St. Ignatius.* Ijamsville, Maryland: The Word Among Us Press, 2002.

Martinez, Marie Louise, RSCJ, Editor. *Southward, Ho! The Society of the Sacred Heart Enters "Lands of the Spanish Sea".* St. Louis: The Society of the Sacred Heart, United States Province, 2003.

Puhl, Louis J., S.J. *The Spiritual Exercises of St. Ignatius.* Chicago: The Newman Press, 1951.

Rahner, Karl, S.J. and Imhof, Paul, S.J. *Ignatius of Loyola.* Original edition published in Germany as *Ignatius von Loyola* in 1978. New York: Collins, 1979.

Tylenda, Joseph N., S.J. *Jesuit Saints & Martyrs.* Chicago: Loyola Press, 1998, pages 403-405.

Williams, Margaret. *Second Sowing: The Life of Mary Aloysia Hardey.* New York: Sheed & Ward, 1942.

Winters, John D. *The Civil War in Louisiana.* Baton Rouge: Louisiana State University Press, 1963.

Magazine and newspaper articles, correspondence and other documents

100th Anniversary of the Convent of the Sacred Heart, Grand Coteau, Louisiana, 1821-1921. (Program from the event)

"A Brief Sketch of the Life and Death of Reverend Michael Arthur Grace, S.J." (Translated from the necrologium, Jesuits' New Orleans Province Archives.) July 28, 1945.

Academy of the Sacred Heart at Grand Coteau Annual Report, 1995-96, page 46.

Adams, Sr. M. Boniface, SSF. Biographical essay on the life of Sr. Jane Frances Evans, a Sister of the Holy Family and longtime principal of Christ the King School in Bellevue, La.

Angers, Trent. "The Canonization of Katharine Drexel." *Acadiana Profile* Magazine. September/October 2000 edition, pages 12-22.

——, "The Miracle of Grand Coteau." *Acadiana Profile* Magazine. May 1976 edition, pages 28-32. (Chapter 3 in this book, titled "The Miracle of Grand Coteau," is a modified version of the article by the author which appeared in the May 1976 edition of *Acadiana Profile.* Also, Chapters 4 and 6 are substantially expanded versions of articles written by the author in *Acadiana Profile's* March/April 2002 edition.)

Bascom, Marion, RSCJ. *Rose Philippine Duchesne: Pioneer Missionary of the New World.* Purchase, New York: Manhattanville College, undated.

Benausse, F., S.J. *Account of the Cure of Miss Mary Wilson, Novice in the Community of the Sacred Heart, Grand Coteau, Louisiana.* (Presented to Most Rev. J.M. Odin, Archbishop of New Orleans; dated February 22, 1867.) Baltimore: John Murphy & Co., 1873.

Biever, Fr. Albert H., S.J. *Reminiscences Of A Southern Jesuit.* New Orleans, 1930. (Unpublished manuscript)

Campbell, Dr. James G. His testimony relative to the illness of Mary Wilson while she was under his care October 19-25, 1866. Document dated January 23, 1867.

Castille, Carl J., S.J. *A Historical Study of St. Charles College.* (Revised Edition, 1961) Grand Coteau: Society of Jesus, New Orleans Province.

Christ the King, Bellevue, La., 1942. A brief history of Christ the King School and Church at Bellevue. Anonymous, unpublished article from the archives of the Sisters of the Holy Family, New Orleans.

Clancy, Fr. Tom, S.J. Brief biography of Fr. Cornelius Thensted, S.J., longtime pastor of Christ the King Church in Grand Coteau.

Coco, Fr. Frank, S.J. "Weekend Miracles." Unpublished manuscript about

Fr. Coco's experiences and observations while serving as a retreat director at Our Lady of the Oaks Retreat House in Grand Coteau.

Doize, Sr. Marie Pamela, RSCJ. "Educational Work of the Society of the Sacred Heart of Jesus in Lower Louisiana, 1821-1930," pages 54-59. Unpublished Master's thesis, St. Louis University, 1930.

Goals and Criteria for Sacred Heart Schools in the United States. Newton, Massachusetts: Network of Sacred Heart Schools, 1990.

Gould, Virginia Meacham and Nolan, Charles E. *Henriette Delille: "Servant of Slaves".* New Orleans: Sisters of the Holy Family, 1999.

"History of Our Lady of the Oaks Retreat House," an undated document in the Director's Office at Our Lady of the Oaks in Grand Coteau.

Jeanmard, Bishop Jules. "Bishop Presents Mission House to Jesuit Order." *The Times-Picayune*, Oct. 2, 1938.

Louapre, Fr. Al, S.J. *History of St. Charles College, Grand Coteau, Louisiana.* Grand Coteau: Society of Jesus, New Orleans Province, undated.

McGill, Fr. Joe, S.J. Retreat lectures, Nov. 1-3, 2002.

McNaspy, Fr. C.J. *The Miracle at Grand Coteau.* Undated booklet.

Millard, Dr. Edward M. His testimony relative to the illness and cure of Mary Wilson while she was under his care October 25 to December 14, 1866. Document dated February 4, 1867.

Minister's Diary of St. Charles College, Grand Coteau, Louisiana. Entries from December of 1837 through December of 1945).

Nachon, Fr. F.M., S.J. Letter to Miss Mary A. Perry of Perry's Bridge, La., dated December 18, 1866 regarding the recent Miracle of Grand Coteau. (From the Jesuits' New Orleans Province Archives, Loyola University, New Orleans)

O'Neal, Fr. Norman B., S.J. *The Life of St. Ignatius of Loyola.* New Orleans: New Orleans Province of Jesuits (Undated)

"Please..." Newsletter, February, 1956, Vol. V No. 4. The newsletter, initiated by Fr. Cornelius Thensted, S.J., was a means of raising funds for the needs of the people and the church parish of Christ the King.

Pope John Paul II. Written statement issued on the occasion of the canonization of Katharine Drexel, October of 2000.

Sampson, Sr. M. Stanislaus, SSF. Biographical essay on the life of Sr. Jane Frances Evans, a Sister of the Holy Family and longtime principal of Christ the King School in Bellevue, La.

"St. Peter Claver School Notes." (From the National Archives of the Society of the Sacred Heart, St. Louis)

Thensted, Fr. Cornelius, S.J. Letter to Lafayette Bishop Jules Jeanmard reporting on the retreats he gave for the black community at Bellevue, dated August 13, 1936. (From the Archives of the Diocese of Lafayette)

————, Letters to Mother Katharine Drexel, SBS, thanking her for her donations to his causes benefiting the black community in the Grand Coteau area, dated May 11, 1939 and December 8, 1939.

————, Letter to potential donors soliciting urgently needed financial help for projects benefiting the black communities of Grand Coteau and Bellevue, dated December 1957. (From the Archives of the New Orleans Province of Jesuits at Loyola University, New Orleans)

Thibodeaux, Charles B., S.J. Homily given at funeral Mass for Sr. Jane Frances Evans (1909-1978), a Sister of the Holy Family and longtime principal of Christ the King School in Bellevue, La. (From a letter dated October 8, 1978, in the Archives of the Sisters of the Holy Family, New Orleans.) Fr. Thibodeaux notes that Sr. Jane Frances spent thirty-five years in Bellevue, and he describes her as "a person totally dedicated (and) committed to the poor, to Christ the King School, bringing Jesus to the needy." He points out that she often overcame extreme financial difficulty: "Financially, often the wolf was at the door. She did not know how she would pay the next teachers' salary or the bills. But then some kind person would send a donation – then she would say, 'God is walking in Bellevue. God is so good.'"

Widman, Fr. C.M., S.J. "Grand Coteau College in War Times." *Woodstock Letters* (Jesuit Magazine) Vol. XXX, 1901, pages 34-49.

Wilson, Mary. Her official attestation relative to her cure in the Miracle of Grand Coteau. Statement given in January of 1867.

Personal Interviews

Arceneaux, Fr. Louis, C.M. Retreat director, Jesuit Spirituality Center in Grand Coteau.

Barry, Willie. Longtime resident of Grand Coteau who grew up across the street from the Jesuit novitiate in the 1930s.

Blish, Sr. Mary, RSCJ. Researcher and editor for the Society of the Sacred Heart, residing in New Orleans.

Broussard, Fr. Warren, S.J. Director of the Jesuit Spirituality Center in Grand Coteau.

Buddendorff, Fr. Kenneth, S.J. Director of Our Lady of the Oaks Retreat House and founder of a program to train lay men and women to be retreat directors at Our Lady of the Oaks.

Burleigh, Darrell. Parish manager of St. Charles Borromeo Church in Grand Coteau.

Burns, Mary. Headmistress of the Academy of the Sacred Heart at Grand Coteau.

Carson, Catharine. Longtime secretary to Fr. Cornelius Thensted, S.J., from 1952 to 1965.

Charles, Mary Louise. Lifelong resident of Grand Coteau and "adopted daughter" of Madame Theresa Bajat Chatrian, a local philanthropist who contributed steadily and heavily to Fr. Thensted's programs to help the local black community.

Coco, Fr. Frank, S.J. Longtime retreat director, Our Lady of the Oaks Retreat House.

Coco, Mayor Jean Jones. Mayor of Grand Coteau (1999 -); former parishioner of Christ the King Church, pastored by Fr. Cornelius Thensted, S.J.; and former volunteer worker on "Please..." newsletter.

Condry, Fr. John, S.J. Longtime retreat director, Our Lady of the Oaks Retreat House.

Downey, Sr. Theresa, RSCJ. Volunteer worker at Thensted Outreach Center.

Dupont, Ronnie. Professional musician (jazz pianist) from New Orleans who credits a retreat at Our Lady of the Oaks, directed by Fr. Frank Coco, S.J., with saving his life.

Edmond, Pauline Ozene. Graduate of St. Peter Claver High School and former parishioner of Christ the King Church, pastored by Fr. Thensted.

Gaulene, Joan. Member of the staff of the archives of the New Orleans Province of Jesuits.

Gavan, Sr. Mary Louise, RSCJ. Member of the staff of the national archives of the Society of the Sacred Heart, St. Louis, Missouri.

Gimber, Sr. Frances, RSCJ. National archivist for the Society of the Sacred Heart, St. Louis, Missouri.

Greiwe, Sr. Marie, RSCJ. Former administrator at the Academy of the Sacred Heart at Grand Coteau. (Interview conducted in April of 1976)

Guidry, Charlie. Longtime resident of Grand Coteau and a professional musician.

Hawkins, Fr. Donald, S.J. Archivist, New Orleans Province of Jesuits.

Henry, Deacon Samuel. Deacon at St. Charles Borromeo Church in Grand Coteau.

Hoffman, Sr. Margaret, RSCJ. Founder and former director of the Thensted Outreach Center in Grand Coteau.

Huete, Fr. Francis W., S.J. Novice director, New Orleans Province of Jesuits.

Jenniskens, Fr. Thomas, S.J. Retreat director, Jesuit Spirituality Center in Grand Coteau; close acquaintance of Fr. Cornelius Thensted, S.J. He knew Fr. Thensted when he (Fr. Thensted) was pastor of Grand Coteau's black church parish and cared for him while in the infirmary at St. Charles College with Alzheimer's.

Key, Julia Eaglin. Lifelong resident of Grand Coteau; graduate of Sacred Heart Colored School; and elementary school teacher for 37 years, now retired.

Kurtz, Sheila. Principal of the high school of the Academy of the Sacred Heart at Grand Coteau.

Landry, Dr. Julie Fontenot. Principal of the elementary school of the Academy of the Sacred Heart, and 1961 graduate of the Academy.

Landry, Ida Jane Coco. Former volunteer worker on "Please..." newsletter; attended St. Peter Claver Elementary in Grand Coteau.

Leslie, Sr. Carolyn. Archivist for the Sisters of the Holy Family, residing in New Orleans.

Louapre, Fr. Al, S.J. Former director of the Jesuit Spirituality Center in Grand Coteau.

Maroney, Lucile Bechet. 1948 graduate of the Academy of the Sacred Heart.

Martin, Felix "Buck" (1912-2004). Lifelong resident of Grand Coteau and graduate of Sacred Heart Colored School.

Martin, Sr. Eva Regina. A Sister of the Holy Family; graduate of St. Peter Claver High School; and former parishioner of Christ the King Church, pastored by Fr. Thensted.

McGill, Fr. Joe, S.J. Longtime retreat director, Our Lady of the Oaks Retreat House.

Meyers, Pauline Pelafigue. Longtime employee of the Academy of the Sacred Heart who lived in a cottage on the grounds of the Academy.

Mills, Sr. Alice, RSCJ. Volunteer worker at Thensted Outreach Center.

Mouton, Sr. Odeide, RSCJ. Former president of Maryville College in St. Louis; and former archivist at the Academy of the Sacred Heart at Grand Coteau. (Interview conducted in April of 1976)

Murphy, Bro. George, S.J. Longtime minister of hospitality at St. Charles College.

Murray, Mary. Former Mayor of Grand Coteau, from 1991 to 1998; attended Sacred Heart Colored School; recipient of scholarship to attend Holy Rosary Institute in Lafayette, La., scholarship having been secured by Fr. Thensted.

Olivier, Julie Brinkhaus. 1946 graduate of the Academy of the Sacred Heart.

Orgeron, Marie Antoinette. 1966 graduate of the Academy of the Sacred Heart.

Phelan, Sr. Margaret, RSCJ. International archivist for the Society of the Sacred Heart, residing in Rome.

Pollingue, Mary Gabriella Logan. 1945 graduate of the College of the Sacred Heart at Grand Coteau.

Renard, Sr. Betty, RSCJ. Volunteer worker at Thensted Outreach Center.

Richard, Julia. Director of the Thensted Outreach Center in Grand Coteau.

Sibille, Jeannie Abshire. 1946 graduate of the Academy of the Sacred Heart.

Tate, John. Longtime groundskeeper and former foreman of the farming operation at St. Charles College.

Welsh, Fr. John, S.J. Retreat director, Jesuit Spirituality Center in Grand Coteau.

Wentworth, Mary. Niece of Fr. Cornelius Thensted, S.J., and resident of New Orleans.

References

Chapter 1. The Character of Grand Coteau

p. 19 – ...*throughout the Western Hemisphere.*: Marie Louise Martinez, *Southward Ho! The Society of the Sacred Heart Enters "Lands of the Spanish Sea,"* pages 145-146.

p. 19 – ... *a deeper relationship with God.*: Fr. Al Louapre, S.J., personal interview.

p. 20 – ...*its original name in 1971.*: Bonnie T. Barry, *A History of the Building of St. Charles Borromeo Catholic Church.*

p. 23 – ...*he succeeded in great measure.*: Sr. Margaret Hoffman and Julia Richard, personal interviews.

p. 23 – ...*grounds of the Academy of the Sacred Heart.*: "St. Peter Claver School Notes," from the National Archives of the Society of the Sacred Heart.

Chapter 2. Academy of the Sacred Heart

p. 31 – ...*These principles are ageless.*: *Goals and Criteria for Sacred Heart Schools in the United States.*

p. 31 – ...*practical and applied.*: Julie F. Fontenot, personal interview.

p. 32 – ...*the world in which they live.*: Sheila Kurtz, personal interview.

pp. 32-37 – ...*A brief history of the Academy of the Sacred Heart*: Louise Callan, RSCJ. *The Society of the Sacred Heart in North America,* pages 112-153.

p. 32 – ...*longer than any other.*: Mary Burns, personal interview.

p. 38 – ...*be spared the destruction of war.*: Louise Callan, RSCJ, *The Society of the Sacred Heart in North America,* page 520.

p. 38 – ...*to honor her request.*: Ibid, pages 528-529.

p. 39 – ...*punished with death.*: Ibid, page 528.

p. 41 – ...*lack of food.*: Ibid.

p. 41 – ...*engaged by the opposition.*: John D. Winters, *The Civil War in Louisiana.*

p. 42 – ...*stronger than it actually was.*: Ibid.

p. 42 – ...*balcony of the Academy.*: Louise Callan, *The Society of the Sacred Heart in North America.*

p. 43 – ...*could not pay them with money.*: Ibid, page 539.

p. 44 – ...*teaching them.*: Ibid

p. 44 – ...*in 1947.*: "St. Peter Claver Notes," from the National Archives of the Society of the Sacred Heart.

pp. 44-47 – ...*An international novitiate.*: Mary Louise Martinez, *Southward Ho! The Society of the Sacred Heart Enters "Lands of the Spanish Sea,"* pages 145-146.

p. 47 – ...*for the occasion.*: Julie Olivier, Marie Orgeron, Lucile Maroney, personal interviews.

p. 49 – ...*do the cooking.*: Ibid.

p. 49 – ...*closed in 1974.*: Marie Orgeron, personal interview.

p. 49 – ...*a little sugar.*: Lucile Maroney, personal interview.

p. 49 – ...*at the pharmacy.*: Jeannie A. Sibille, personal interview.

p. 49 – ...*watchful eye of the nuns.*: Julie Olivier, personal interview.

p. 49 – ...*all-girls Catholic school.*: Lucile Maroney, personal interview.

p. 50 – ...*local church communities.*: Mary Burns, personal interview.

p. 50 – ...*in the 1960s.*: Julie F. Landry, personal interview.

p. 50 – ...*through the 1960s.*: Lucile Maroney, personal interview.

p. 51 – ...*around the world.*: Marie Orgeron, personal interview.

p. 51 – ...*to help shape our new world.*: Mona Cravins, *Academy of the Sacred Heart at Grand Coteau Annual Report, 1995-96,* page 46.

Chapter 3. The Miracle of Grand Coteau

p. 54 – ...*take her back to Canada...*: Sr. Marie Greiwe, personal interview.

pp. 55-61 – ...*Mary Wilson's illness and cure.*: Fr. F. Benausse, *Account of the Cure of Mary Wilson...*; Fr. C.J. McNaspy, *The Miracle at Grand Coteau*; and attestations of Mary Wilson, Dr. Edward M. Millard and Dr. James G. Campbell.

p. 55 – ...*disease of the stomach.*: Dr. James Campbell's attestation.

p. 57 – ...*given up hope...*: Dr. Edward Millard's attestation.

p. 59 – ...*"neither I nor my prescriptions..."*: Ibid.

p. 61 – ...*die before her noviceship ended.*: Fr. C.J. McNaspy, *The Miracle at Grand Coteau,* page 28.

Chapter 4. St. Charles College

p. 65 – ...*primary mission of the center.*: Fr. Al Louapre, personal interview.

p. 67 – ...*New Orleans Provincial Office.*: Ibid.

pp. 67-69 – ...*St. Charles College functions as a novitiate.*: Fr. Francis Huete, personal interview.

pp. 70-77 – ...*A school for boys and young men.*: *Minister's Diary of St. Charles College,* 1838-1922; Fr. C.M. Widman, "Grand Coteau College in War Times," *Woodstock Letters,* Vol. XXX, 1901, pages 34-49; Fr. Albert Biever, *Reminiscences of a Southern Jesuit*; Fr. Al Louapre, *History of St. Charles College*; and Fr. Carl Castille, *A Historical Study of St. Charles College.*

p. 70 – ...*untamed reaches of Louisiana.*: Fr. Al Louapre, *History of St. Charles College.*

p. 72 – ...*Jesuits headed for Grand Coteau.*: Louise Callan, *The Society of the Sacred Heart in North America,* pages 150-151.

p. 72 – ...*a junior college.*: Fr. Al Louapre, *History of St. Charles College.*

p. 73 – ...*send their children to the college.*: *Minister's Diary,* July 1943.

p. 73 – ...*Civil War in 1861.*: Ibid, April, 1861.

p. 73 – ...*all its citizens.*: Fr. C.M. Widman, "Grand Coteau College in War Times," *Woodstock Letters,* Vol. XXX, 1901.

p. 73 – ...*attending Mass.*: Ibid.

p. 74 – ...*second-story balcony.*: Ibid, and Louise Callan, *The Society of the Sacred Heart in North America.*

p. 75 – ...*the dreaded fever...*: *Minister's Diary,* Oct. 1867.

p. 75 – ...*returned to Alabama.*: Fr. Al Louapre, *History of St. Charles College.*

p. 76 – ...*another fire...*: Ibid.

p. 77 – ...*financial debilitation and stress.*: Ibid.

pp. 77-81 – *A novitiate for the training of Jesuit priests and brothers.*: Fr. Francis Huete, personal interviews; Fr. Thomas Jenniskens, personal interviews; Fr. Al Louapre, *History of St. Charles College*; and John Tate (longtime employee of St. Charles College), personal interview.

p. 78 – ...*humanistic studies.*: Fr. Francis Huete, personal interview.

p. 78 – ...*priests living in the house.*: Fr. Thomas Jenniskens, personal interview.

p. 78 – ...*sold for cash.*: Ibid.

p. 78 – ...*seldom left the property.*: Ibid

p. 81 – ...*novices would trudge out of the fields...*: Ibid, and John Tate, personal interview.

pp. 81-84 – ...*The Great Flood of 1927.*: "A Brief Sketch of the Life and Death of Rev. Michael Arthur Grace, S.J." from the Archives of the New Orleans Province of Jesuits; and Glenn R. Conrad, *Crevasse! The 1927 Flood in Acadiana*; and *Minister's Diary*, 1927.

p. 82 – ...*scrambling for higher ground.*: Glenn R. Conrad, *Crevasse! The 1927 Flood in Acadiana*.

p. 82 – ...*massive relief effort.*: "A Brief Sketch of the Life and Death of Rev. Michael Arthur Grace, S.J."

p. 84 – ...*a facility...exclusively for retreats...*: Fr. Al Louapre, *History of St. Charles College*.

p. 86 – ...*a golden era for Jesuits...*: Ibid.

p. 87 – ...*spirituality of their founders.*: Fr. Francis Huete and Fr. Thomas Jenniskens, personal interviews.

Chapter 5. St. Ignatius and the Spiritual Exercises

pp. 91-95 – ...*Biography of St. Ignatius Loyola.*: Fr. Norman O'Neal, *The Life of St. Ignatius Loyola*; and Fr. Karl Rahner and Fr. Paul Imhof, *Ignatius of Loyola*.

pp. 95-99 – ...*The Spiritual Exercises.*: Fr. Louis Arceneaux, Fr. Ken Buddendorff, Fr. Francis Huete, Fr. Al Louapre and Fr. John Welsh, personal interviews; and Fr. Manuel Ruiz Jurado, *For the Greater Glory of God: A Spiritual Retreat with St. Ignatius*.

p. 98 – ..."*God's deepening his life in me.*": Fr. David Fleming, *Draw Me Into Your Friendship: The Spiritual Exercises – A Literal Translation and a Contemporary Reading*.

Chapter 6. Our Lady of the Oaks Retreat House

p. 103 – "...*beehive of spiritual activity.*": Bishop Jules Jeanmard, "Bishop Presents Mission House To Jesuit Order," *The Times-Picayune*, Oct. 2, 1938.

p. 103 – ...*funding for the facility...*: "History of Our Lady of the Oaks Retreat House," undated document, from the Director's Office of Our Lady of the Oaks.

p. 104 – ...*based on the Spiritual Exercises...*: Fr. Kenneth Buddendorff, personal interview.

pp. 105-108 – '*Weekend Miracles.*': Fr. Frank Coco, personal interviews and unpublished manuscript.

p. 107 – "...*nor am I afraid to be alone.*": Ronnie Dupont, personal interview.

p. 108 – ...*help staff this ministry.*: Fr. Kenneth Buddendorff, personal interview.

p. 109 – "...*retreat movement is growing.*": Fr. John Condry, personal interview.

Chapter 7. Coming Home...

p. 112 – *"...we can only babble."*: "Dynamic of the Retreat: Silence," literature in each retreatant's room at Our Lady of the Oaks.

pp. 116-119 – *...natural and supernatural programming...*: Fr. Joe McGill, retreat lectures, Nov. 1-3, 2002.

p. 117 – *"...our reality and our hope..."*: Ibid.

p. 119 – *"...maximalist position...true Christianity..."*: Ibid.

Chapter 8. A Convergence of Saints

p. 121 – *...and again in 1829.*: Louise Callan, *The Society of the Sacred Heart in North America.*

p. 122 – *"...noblest and most virtuous..."*: Msgr. Peter Richard Kenrick, Archbishop of St. Louis.

p. 122 – *...requests from Jesuit priests...*: Fr. A.B. Fox and Fr. Michael Grace, both of whom resided at St. Charles College, are among the Jesuit priests who asked for and received donations for worthy causes for the black community from Mother Katharine Drexel. The letters from these priests, written in 1916 and 1925, are stored in the Sisters of the Blessed Sacrament's National Archives in Bensalem, Penn. Mother Katharine donated to similar causes backed by the legendary Fr. Cornelius Thensted.

p. 122 – *...visited the Sacred Heart Colored School...*: Sr. F. Savorelli, RSCJ, living at the Academy of the Sacred Heart at Grand Coteau, wrote Mother Katharine Drexel on Feb. 27, 1921, thanking her for the visit she made to the Sacred Heart Colored School, on the grounds of the Academy.

p. 124 – *"...a more just and fraternal world."*: Pope John Paul II, in a written statement he issued on the occasion of the canonization of Katharine Drexel, in October of 2000. (The canonization was attended by the author.)

p. 124 – *...his canonization in 1888.*: Fr. Joseph Tylenda, *Jesuit Saints & Martyrs*, pages 403-405.

p. 124 – *...lived on the grounds of the Academy...*: Louise Callan, *The Society of the Sacred Heart in North America;* and Margaret Williams, *Second Sowing: The Life of Mary Aloysia Hardey.*

p. 125 – *"...highest expression of God's mercy and love."*: Society of the Holy Child Jesus, a brief biography of Mother Connelly.

pp. 126-127 – *Henriette Delille...*: Virginia M. Gould and Charles E. Nolan, *Henriette Delille, "Servant of Slaves."*

Chapter 9. Fr. Thensted, Sr. Mike...

p. 129 – *"...an icon of social justice."*: Sr. Eva Regina Martin, personal interview.

p. 130 – *Fr. Thensted's biography, 1903-1936.*: Fr. Tom Clancy wrote a biographical sketch of the life of Fr. Thensted after his death in 1981; it is stored in the Jesuit Archives at Loyola University in New Orleans.

p. 132 – *...reaching out to educate black children...*: Louise Callan, *The Society of the Sacred Heart in North America.*

p. 132 – *…children came…on foot…*: Felix "Buck" Martin, Julia E. Key and Mary Louise Charles, personal interviews.

p. 133 – *…taught…by Jesuit Scholastics…*: A brief, unpublished history of Christ the King School and Church, titled "Christ the King, Bellevue, La.," in the archives of the Sisters of the Holy Family in New Orleans.

p. 133 – *…700 people attended.*: Fr. Cornelius Thensted, in a letter to Lafayette Bishop Jules Jeanmard, Aug. 13, 1936.

p. 133 – *…send some of their sisters…*: History of Christ the King School and Church, Sisters of the Holy Family archives.

p. 133 – *…a new, larger convent…*: Ibid.

p. 133 – *…the school's first principal…*: Sr. M. Boniface Adams and Sr. M. Stanislaus Sampson both wrote brief biographical sketches of Sr. Jane Frances Evans, which are stored in the archives of the Sisters of the Holy Family.

p. 133 – *…economically and educationally…*": Sr. Eva Regina Martin, personal interview.

p. 134 – *…a new St. Peter Claver School…*: "St. Peter Claver School Notes," National Archives of the Society of the Sacred Heart.

p. 134 – *…need for teaching staff was created…*: Sr. Theresa Downey, personal interview.

p. 135 – "*…He was completely dedicated…*": Julia Richard, Sr. Eva Regina Martin and Ida Jane Coco Landry, personal interviews.

p. 136 – *…up at 3:30 or 4…*: Fr. Tom Jenniskens, personal interview.

p. 136 – *…he spoke loudly…*: Ida Jane Coco Landry and Julia Richard, personal interviews.

p. 136 – *…he did have detractors.*: Catharine Carson and Fr. Tom Jenniskens, personal interviews.

p. 136 – *…tended to awaken the Jesuits…*: Fr. Tom Jenniskens, personal interview.

p. 136 – *…until 10:30 or 11…*: Catharine Carson, personal interview.

p. 136 – *…the way he wore his clothes…*: Fr. Tom Jenniskens, Ida Jane Coco Landry and Julia Richard, personal interviews.

p. 136 – *…deeply religious and spiritual man…*: Fr. Tom Jenniskens and Sr. Eva Regina Martin, personal interviews.

p. 137 – *…go into the church with his staff…*: Catharine Carson, personal interview.

p. 137 – *…visit the children…*: Fr. Tom Clancy, biographical sketch of the life of Fr. Thensted.

p. 137 – *…demanded…they behave respectfully…*: Ida Jane Coco Landry and Julia Richard, personal interviews.

p. 137 – *…a tendency to give advice…*: Ibid.

p. 137 – *…finished with the classroom…*: Fr. Tom Jenniskens, personal interview.

p. 137 – *…he secured financial aid…*: Mary Murray and Pauline O. Edmond, personal interviews.

p. 137 – *…he helped…Mary Murray…*: Mary Murray, personal interview.

p. 138 – *…a more challenging line of work…*: Pauline O. Edmond, personal interview.

p. 138 – *…pitching in to get things done.*: Sr. Alice Mills and Julia Richard, personal interviews.

p. 138 – *…newsletter titled "Please…"*: Ida Jane Coco Landry, Mary Murray and Julia Richard, personal interviews.

p. 139 – *…appealed…to Mother Katharine Drexel…*: Fr. Cornelius Thensted, letters to Mother Katharine, 1938 and 1939.

p. 140 – *…Madame Theresa Bajat Chatrian…*: Catharine Carson, Fr. Francis Huete and Mary Wentworth, personal interviews.

p. 141 – *...the people in his care.*: Catharine Carson, personal interview.

p. 141 – *...unwelcome visit from two town officials*: Ibid.

p. 141 – *...a just and honorable man.*: Ibid.

p. 142 – *...do his spiritual work.*: Ibid.

p. 142 – *...a petition was circulated...*: Ibid.

p. 142 – *...disapproved of his efforts...*: Ibid.

p. 142 – *...a policeman stopped the truck...*: Jean Jones Coco, personal interview.

p. 143 – *...Fr. Thensted was worn out.*: Fr. Tom Jenniskens, personal interview.

pp. 143-147 – *Sr. Margaret Hoffman's tenure in Grand Coteau*: Sr. Margaret Hoffman, a series of personal interviews.

p. 147 – *Fr. Thensted died...*: Fr. Tom Clancy, biographical sketch of the life of Fr. Thensted.

Index

Note: All references in **bold** refer to photographs or illustrations.

Photo, Art and Map Credits

Ancona, Charles (New Iberia, La.) – 14 (church), 18 (Fr. Coco), 100, 102, 107, 109, 116, back end sheet

Angers, Trent (Lafayette, La.) – 22, 60, 62, 66 (Fr. Jim Dolan), 114, 115

Bell, Elizabeth (Lafayette, La.) – Maps on pages 24, 25

Bonwili, C.E.H. (Civil War art appeared in *Frank Leslie's Illustrated Newspaper* on Dec. 12, 1863; art courtesy of Archives Dept., University of Louisiana - Lafayette Library) – 39

Camel, Nancy (Baton Rouge, La.) – 40, 41, 85

Carson, Catharine (Girard, Ohio) – 139

Darling, Diane (Development Office, Academy of the Sacred Heart, Grand Coteau) – 19 (girls with cat), 21 (teacher with student), 28, 29, 46, 48

Dickens, James (New Iberia, La.) – 18 (Felix Martin), 19 (Julia Key), 20 (Willie Barry)

Doehling, Susan (Back in Time Photography, Lafayette, La.) – 12, 14 (Pietá), 15, 17, 88, 89, 120, front end sheet

Fuselier, Dr. John (Lafayette, La.) – 26

Izzo, Danny (*Nouveau Photeau*, Lafayette, La.) – 42, 43, 61, 110

Milligan, Wes (Lafayette, La.) – 104 (Statue of St. John Berchmans)

Perdrau, Pauline (Society of the Sacred Heart, Rome) – 45

Sisters of the Blessed Sacrament Archives, Bensalem, Penn. – 123

Sisters of the Holy Family Archives, New Orleans, La. – 126

Society of Jesus Archives, New Orleans Province, Loyola University, New Orleans – 64, 71, 75, 79, 80, 82, 83, 86, 130, 131, 134, 135

Society of Jesus Novitiate, New Orleans Province, Grand Coteau, La. – 20 (Mr. Nguyen and Sr. Fontenot), 68, 69

Society of the Holy Child Jesus Archives, Rosemont, Penn. – 125

Society of the Sacred Heart Archives, St. Louis – 33, 34, 36, 45, 122

Thensted Outreach Center, Grand Coteau, La. – 128, 143

About the Author

TRENT ANGERS, who was nominated twice for the Nobel Prize in Literature (2000 and 2001), is a veteran journalist who has authored thousands of published news and feature stories, as well as four books, in a writing and editing career that has spanned four decades.

His books are: *The Truth About The Cajuns* (1989); *Dudley LeBlanc: A Biography* (1993); *The Forgotten Hero Of My Lai: The Hugh Thompson Story* (1999); and *Grand Coteau: The Holy Land of South Louisiana* (2004).

A member of the Secular Franciscan Order, he was schooled by the Christian Brothers at Hanson Memorial High School in Franklin, La., graduating in 1966.

He received a Bachelor of Arts degree from Louisiana State University in 1970 and was named the Outstanding Graduating Senior in Journalism by Sigma Delta Chi, a professional journalism organization. He also won the Hodding Carter Award for Responsible Journalism. He served an apprenticeship at *The Palm Beach (Florida) Post*. In the early 1970s he was a staff correspondent for *The Times-Picayune* of New Orleans and *The Beaumont Enterprise*.

Since 1975, Angers has been editor and publisher of *Acadiana Profile*, "The Magazine of the Cajun Country," based in Lafayette, La.; it is one of the longest-running regional publications in the United States.

Inspiring Books
from
ACADIAN HOUSE PUBLISHING

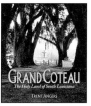

Grand Coteau
The Holy Land of South Louisiana

A 176-page hardcover book that captures the spirit of one of the truly holy places in North America. It is a town of mystery, with well-established ties to the supernatural, including the famous Miracle of Grand Coteau. Brought to life by dozens of exceptional color photographs, the book focuses on the town's major religious institutions: The Academy of the Sacred Heart, Our Lady of the Oaks Retreat House and St. Charles College/ Jesuit Spirituality Center. The book explores not only the history of these three institutions but also the substance of their teachings. (Author: Trent Angers. ISBN: 0-925417-47-5. Price: $44.95)

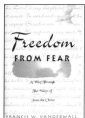

Freedom From Fear
A Way Through The Ways of Jesus The Christ

Everyone at one time or another feels fear, guilt, worry and shame. But when these emotions get out of control they can enslave a person, literally taking over his or her life. In this 142-page hardcover book, the author suggests that the way out of this bondage is prayer, meditation and faith in God and His promise of salvation. The author points to the parables in the Gospels as Jesus' antidote to fears of various kinds, citing the parables of the prodigal son, the good Samaritan, and the widow and the judge. Exercises at the end of each chapter help make the book's lessons all the more real and useful. (Author: Francis Vanderwall. ISBN: 0-925417-34-3. Price: $14.95)

Water From Stones
An Inner Journey

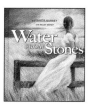

Water From Stones is a 128-page hardcover book that is designed to serve as an instrument of healing, renewal and enlightenment for those who are seeking to walk a spiritual path. It is a book for those who are willing to take positive steps toward a more meaningful, more joyful life. The author maintains that the events and circumstances that test our hearts and spirits can bring forth our greatest gifts. She points out that spiritual and psychological healing comes to us as we learn and accept what she refers to as "the lessons of the desert." (Author: Lyn Doucet. ISBN: 0-925417-40-8. Price: $12.95.)

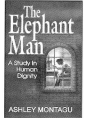

The Elephant Man
A Study in Human Dignity

The Elephant Man is a 138-page softcover book whose first edition inspired the movie and the Tony Award-winning play by the same name. This fascinating story, which has touched the hearts of readers throughout the world for over a century, is now complete with the publication of this, the Third Edition. Illustrated with photos and drawings of The Elephant Man. (Author: Ashley Montagu. ISBN: 0-925417-41-6. Price: $12.95.)

The Forgotten Hero of My Lai
The Hugh Thompson Story

A 248-page hardcover book that tells the story of the U.S. Army helicopter pilot who risked his life to rescue South Vietnamese civilians and to put a stop to the My Lai massacre during the Vietnam War in 1968. An inspiring story about the courage to do the right thing under extremely difficult circumstances, regardless of the consequences. Illustrated with maps and photos. (Author: Trent Angers. ISBN: 0-925417-33-5. Price: $22.95)

TO ORDER, list the books you wish to purchase along with the corresponding cost of each. Add $3 per book for shipping & handling. Louisiana residents add 8% tax to the cost of the books. Mail your order and check or credit card authorization (VISA/MC/AmEx) to: Acadian House Publishing, Dept. B-40, Box 52247, Lafayette, LA 70505. Or call (800) 850-8851.